My name is Ben, and I'm a ~~Nurse~~ Addict

Benjamin D. Cox

authorHOUSE®

AuthorHouse™
1663 Liberty Drive
Bloomington, IN 47403
www.authorhouse.com
Phone: 1-800-839-8640

Published by AuthorHouse 03/16/2016

ISBN: 978-1-4772-1057-4 (sc)
ISBN: 978-1-4772-1055-0 (hc)
ISBN: 978-1-4772-1056-7 (e)

Library of Congress Control Number: 2012909189

Print information available on the last page.

My name is Ben, and I'm a . . .

Son . . .

Brother . . .

Father . . .

Husband . . .

Nurse . . .

Convicted Felon . . .

Addict.

Contents

This book is dedicated to my friends and family who I want to read it, to my wonderful grandfather who I'm glad never has to read it, to my precious daughter who I fear one day will read it . . .
and to me, for having the courage to write it.

Prologue

I am writing to save my life; it's the only thing that helps, like therapy in a way. I feel like a nurse again with a critical patient, but there is no doctor on call, and the patient is myself with severe chest pain. The computer desk is my stretcher, coffee is my nitro spray, cigarettes are my 02, and my pen is my IV. No morphine to numb the pain anymore though. My journal is my ECG and rhythm shows ventricular fibrillation. The laptop is my crash cart . . . clear . . . c'mon Ben . . . ECG still shows in v-fib . . . clear . . . /\ . . . /\ . . . /\ . . . normal sinus rhythm . . . he's OK . . . you're . . . OK . . . it's OK. Your family is here Ben, it's over now and you're going to be alright . . . I'm going to be alright . . .

Foreword

I am alone.
I am not a good person.
I do not recognize who I am anymore.
I am not happy.
I think I am in control; I am not.
I tell myself I am not an addict, I am.
I know I will get caught, but I do not stop.
I will lose my job, my career, my marriage and the trust of my colleagues.
I will get caught. I will lose everything.
I have been caught. I have lost everything.
The weight has lifted, finally. It feels good to talk, for people to know.
I have lost everything only to find myself.
No more pretending, no more lying, no having to stay ahead of everyone.
No more self-hatred.
I am not alone.
I am a good person.
I am happy again.
Be truthful with yourself, and you will realize you like who you are.
I was not happy with my life, my marriage, what I was pretending to be,
and that caused emptiness in my heart.
I will not make addiction my excuse for what I chose to do.
I was depressed and I used drugs to forget how unhappy I was.
I do not need drugs to be happy but I need to be honest with myself
I am strong, I will get better, and I will turn this into a positive experience.
This is my second chance, a fresh start, and a new chapter.
Love yourself, be strong, and stay honest with yourself.
One day at a time, one foot in front of the other, always forward.

-Benjamin Dan Cox, July 8, 2011, Inuvik, Northwest Territories
(Written the day following my suspension)

"Life isn't about finding yourself, it's about creating yourself."
-Anonymous

Introduction

As far as being a financial supporter to my daughter, I was dependable. As far as being a father to her, I was inadequate. As far as being a lover to my wife, I excelled. As far as being a husband to her, I was lacking. As far as being successful in my career, I had been. As far as being happy with my life, I was not. As far as being a nurse, I was selfless. As far as being an addict, I was selfish. And as far as being a writer, I need to be truthful.

It is simply impossible to protect everyone from getting hurt when I write a book like this. I am not a malicious person and I will do everything in my power to write this book with respectfulness, empathy, and class, but there will take a certain amount of selfishness to write it the way that it must be written. I have to do this for me because I am not well these days and writing this book is my only way of healing. Just like talking in my rehab group and in Narcotics Anonymous meetings, writing this book is my therapy. The only difference is that the turnout for this meeting is much larger than the ones that I attended in the basement of a church.

What I am adamant about however, is protecting my loved ones from the harmful effects of such a personal, brutally honest, tell-all book such as this one. For that reason, I have changed the names of certain people who I refuse to let suffer any more because of something I have done.

I have changed the names of my daughter, my wife, my wife's mother and stepfather, my parents, and the clients and staff at the treatment center. I have received permission from all my friends to use their first names in the book so these names are real.

Also, it is known whom I worked with while at the hospital in Inuvik, Northwest Territories (NWT), and their statements as well as mine are all now public record in the Court of the NWT. They have provided sworn statements to the RCMP as well as read several victim impact statements in open court. I addition to this, they have given statements to the media and to the private investigators of the hospital.

Many, including my Nurse Manager, have added their unfounded and speculator opinions about how I managed to use drugs for so long without it being noticed. Therefore, if they can give their opinions of me for the public to hear, then I certainly feel I have the right to give my opinions as well. But I will only respond to what was actually said and recorded by these people, as I have to be aware of liability issues.

I have consulted with an attorney and I have been well informed of what I can get away with saying and what is off limits. So with that being said, my name is Ben and I need to tell my story.

I am not perfect, far from it. I have been pretending to be content with my life for so long that I have forgotten what it really feels like to be happy. I violated my self-integrity so many times that I lost any self-worth I had. I needed help, I needed to talk to someone, anyone. But I could not because I would lose everything I had worked so hard for, my marriage, my career, my freedom . . . everything.

I was a respected Registered Nurse (RN) who worked in the isolated town of Inuvik, NWT. I was seen as a caring, trusted, reliable, competent nurse who worked in the ER for almost 4 years. I am a loving father of a beautiful little girl and husband to a wonderful woman who I have never been in love with but have never had the courage to tell her.

I have been using and addicted to narcotics for over two years, of which I had unlimited access. I know I am not well and need help but I cannot ask for it. Weeks turn into months, months into years, and no one ever notices. And then it happens. I am caught.

Finally, it feels good to talk and for people to know what I have been holding in for so long. I admit to everything and it feels so good when I do that I continue to be honest with everyone. I do not hold back. I tell the RCMP, my parents, my wife, and all my closest friends that I have not been myself for some time and that I am an addict whose life has become unmanageable.

I am arrested and charged. I lose my license to practice. I tell my wife I am not happy with our marriage. I attend a 30-day treatment program for professionals with addiction where I learn to stop helping others and start to help myself. I start journaling and remember how much I used to enjoy writing.

I fly back to Inuvik to face the consequences of my actions and show my true character before the community, the hospital, and the judge. I need them to see who I really am. I do not want to be defined by this one mistake but rather by how I have dealt with it. This makes me feel proud. I like myself again. I am a good person. I am happy with who I am again. I do not know what the consequences will be but I am not scared. I am ready for the judge's decision and I know I will be okay. I have so much support and I am ready to start a new chapter in my life.

I talk without thinking now and hide nothing from the court. I feel relieved when I finish and I have pled guilty from the start because it feels right. No longer do I have to try and stay ahead of everyone. Finally, I can just be myself and talk without hesitation.

I am asked to sit as the judge is going to make a decision as to what my sentence will be. I tell him I would rather stand and I hold my head high. I am ready. I am an addict. I am a good father. I am no longer a nurse. I am just a man whose darkest secrets are there for all to see.

As I stand there I remember my grandfather who passed away and that through my veins flow the blood of a fisherman, hunter, and storyteller, who made his living from the ocean. I remember my parents who are both nurses and I look at my mother, who flew up north to be with me, as she cries. I whisper to her "I love you; I'm sorry". I face the judge. I am at peace. I am just a man. I am ready.

This is my story. I could not have talked about this without going to the treatment program and learning to talk about my feelings and my mistakes. This is all truth and can be proven.

Facing the community, the hospital, and telling others about the terrible mistakes I had made was the hardest thing I had ever done. It has also been the most rewarding and I have found that most people can relate to making mistakes, as we are all imperfect to some degree. We are all human.

I was so good at helping others that I began to ignore myself. This caused me to do things that were against my moral beliefs but I could not stop because it made me forget that I was so unhappy. This cannot be allowed to happen again. Talk to someone. Be honest with yourself. I had to lose so many things that I thought were important to realize that the most important thing is to be happy in the skin I am in. Once we can obtain that, everything else will fall into place. One day at a time.

The Truth
Chapter 1

The truth! As children most of us were taught to always tell it and we quickly found out from our parents, or at least mine anyway, that there were consequences when we did not. While growing up I quickly learned that it always felt better to be truthful about things although I did frequently push my luck and create versions of the truth.

At the time, this seemed like a good idea and less likely to result in punishment than the whole truth surely would. However, the guilt and shame that one would experience immediately after lying was often far worse than any punishment I could have received.

My parents always said they would rather be told the truth than to be lied to regardless of how awful the truth seemed. That moment when the truth came out, more so by means other than my admission, I remember feeling utter relief as a tremendous weight was lifted from my shoulders.

I felt good about myself again and not ashamed anymore. No longer did I have to think ahead of what to say so as to not get caught in my own lies. Instead, I was able to speak freely, feel relaxed, and know that I was a better person for being honest even if it was about something wrong I had done.

So for those people dealing with depression and/or addiction or just pretending to be content with a life that deep inside you know you are not happy with, there is happiness within. I know because I have found it. It has cost me everything I thought was important to find but I have rediscovered what I felt as a child in happier times and I never want to let it go. Better than any drug, one simple thing can change your whole perspective on life. By discovering it and letting it lead you rather than hiding from it you can gain the most important thing there is, self-worth. The simple thing that will lead you to this is truth. Complete honesty with yourself and what you are feeling. You are not alone. There is no worse feeling than not liking who you are and dark things always follow.

For those of you reading this I want to make you a promise. I want to promise to tell the truth. This is not a fictional book and all the contents are actual experiences from my life that I want to share with others. I am doing this not only with the hopes of healing myself and aiding in my own recovery but also to reach others who are dealing with something similar in their lives.

Though I am no longer nursing and my license to practice has been suspended, I still feel I should maintain the confidentiality of the patients that were in my care. I will not mention any of them by name, nor can I go into detail about why they were seen in the ER, as it would easily identify them.

Who I am, what I have done, whom I worked with, and what I have been through, however, is now public knowledge and can be easily obtained from the Territorial Court. I have pled guilty to what I had been doing and fully disclosed every detail to my family, friends, hospital investigators, RCMP, addiction councilors, and to the court on the day of my sentencing.

With that being said, I want to continue on this path of honesty and I am ready to share with you, the reader, the events that led up to my continuing recovery from drug addiction.

Since this is my book I can pretty much talk about what I want so I will briefly tell you about my favorite shows on television (please be patient for those of you wondering where this is going). I love most series on HBO with The Sopranos being my all-time favorite. But every now and then a show comes along that one can relate to on a personal level where you can see yourself being portrayed by actors with an uncanny familiarity (and no, I am not in the mafia). I am referring to another series on HBO, which stars the same actress that plays Tony Soprano's wife, Carmella.

The show is called Nurse Jackie, which centers on the life of the main character, Jackie, who struggles to try and find a balance between her family obligations as a parent, her duties as an ER nurse, and her addiction with prescription narcotics.

It would seem myself and Jackie has much in common. Both of us work in the high stress and fast pace environment of the ER. Like her I am excellent at what I do. Like her I am a parent and I am married. And regrettably, like her, I am addicted to narcotics.

Until recently, no one has ever known this about me, and for almost two years I have kept this a dark secret that I could not tell anyone. Neither my parents, friends, the nurses and physicians I worked closely with, nor my wife, had any idea that I was stealing drugs from work and injecting them into my body for over two years. I simply could not tell them. The shame and guilt would be too much to bear as everyone thought so highly of me. And I could not stop. Immediately after I injected myself I was already planning how to obtain the next one. "One is too many and a thousand never enough", as they tell us in recovery. That statement could not be more accurate. I knew something was wrong with me and I was not well; I could feel it. But I had this feeling long before I began using narcotics, and long before I moved up North.

I try and remember when I was happy last. When I was married perhaps to the woman I had been with for over eight years? The answer is no. Maybe when my child was born which should be the happiest moment in every father's life? The answer again is no. Why cannot I remember feeling happy? I have a great job that I am good at and pays well, a beautiful home, a beautiful wife, a gorgeous little girl, and supportive parents. I am educated, in good physical health, good looking, caring, friendly, and funny . . . so why is it that I cannot remember for the life of me when I was last happy? I try and think back further to when I was young and life was less complicated. I need to remember when I stopped being content with my life.

Some of my fondest memories are of when I was a child growing up in the small town of St. Anthony, Newfoundland (NL), Canada. I was happy there, at least until that day when my life turned upside down, and everything changed. It was the worst day of my life. Worse than losing my license to practice, than being arrested, than going to recovery, or standing before a judge facing jail time. And I have not been the same since.

'Back Home'
Chapter 2

I lived in Nova Scotia (NS), Canada, for almost twelve years. I attended university there, my wife is from there, my daughter was born and raised there, and we bought a home there. NS is where I started my career as a RN working in different hospital settings for over three years until we made our move to the North. My mom lived and worked there as a professor of Nursing for over twelve years, and my dad and stepmom, both of whom work in the healthcare field, moved there with their two daughters almost ten years ago. I should call this home. But for some reason when someone asks me where I am from, I usually respond with the same answer; I am from NL. And when I am asked, "What part of Newfoundland?" I always smile and proudly tell them, St. Anthony.

It has been almost twenty years since I moved away from St. Anthony but I have never forgotten how much I loved it. I will never forget how happy I was there and nothing compares to how painful it was to have to leave. The best years of my life and the worst day of my life took place there, in the small community located at the tip of NL's Northern Peninsula.

I was born on January 2, 1981, in London, Ontario (ON), and was only a few hours shy of being a New Year baby. Mom tells me it was a long hard labor and that I simply "refused to leave". Also, she really wanted the gift basket that mothers receive if their baby is born on New Year's Day. I do not remember anything about my place of birth as my parents moved from ON to NL when I was just four months old. A year and a half later my younger brother Jeff was born making him the only authentic "Newfie" out of our family of four.

Both my parents tell me they loved NL, however, due to a shortage of nursing jobs, our stay there only lasted eight years. I was three and Jeff was only a year old when we moved to Dad's home community of Harrington Harbour, a small island located on the Lower North Shore of Quebec (QC), Canada. Harrington Harbour or "back home" as Dad would say, is one of those special places that you have to see to believe and I often have a hard time describing to people how beautiful it is there.

This tiny island is one of the last thriving fishing communities along the coast and to the 400 or so people that live here, including most of Dad's family, it has been a place where the sea provides a livelihood to those who are willing to work hard and has done so for many generations. It is also the only other place in the world besides St. Anthony where I always feel at home.

These days more and more tourists are making the trip to Harrington to see with their own eyes the beauty that this village has to offer and to breath in the fresh ocean air blowing off the sea that surrounds it from every direction. Several years ago a French film crew used this location to film a movie that happened to be quite successful. When viewers discovered that the charming village on the island really existed, its popularity grew.

The film La Grande Séduction is about a small village that is in competition with other communities trying to get a fish plant established. However, one of the conditions they need fulfilled before they can be considered, is to have a full-time doctor residing there. The villagers proceed to try and "seduce" a big city physician to stay by pretending to have and enjoy all the same interests that he has, which they find out by tapping his phone. In the end the physician falls in love with the community and its people just as many of those who ever visited Harrington have done.

My two uncles and my cousin who currently reside in Harrington Harbour have long taken over the fishing license and the boat The Cape Airey that my grandfather passed over when he could no longer fish. I know he was proud to see them continue with a way of life that he loved so much, one that provided for him and his family for many years.

To try and put into words how special my late grandfather was I would need to dedicate an entirely separate book to him and his many experiences. Entries from the journal he kept as a seal fisherman from 1957-1977 were, in fact, published under the title Seal Fishery Diaries.

A gentleman by the name of Fred Pratson, author of a book called The Sea in their Blood, described him best. He got to know my grandfather, or "Papa", as I call him, by spending a few days with him and he wrote the following excerpt next to a picture of Papa while he was mending his fishing nets. It reads, and I quote:

"He is a man's man; his life is not for those who are weak or lazy. He is an expert mariner, fisherman, sealer, trapper, hunter, storyteller, family man and citizen. He can fix what goes wrong in his home or at sea. He is his own boss and master of his own time. He also shares with most inshore fisherman, courage, self-reliance, mastery of various crafts, good judgment, & an adventurous spirit. He is one of a breed of men who are rare in a more sophisticated society, but one who can be readily found along the rugged North Eastern coast. The survival of their families, communities, and way of life depends on their being who they are, and nothing less"—Fred Pratson.

During the time we lived in Harrington both my parents were nurses in the small outpost clinic that was also equipped with a living area and this is what we called home for two years. I was five when Mom was offered a position as a Public Health Nurse back in NL and even though they loved Harrington the opportunity for a full time position doing what she loved was too much to pass up. So, only two years after leaving NL we were once again moving back there. I was fortunate to be too young to remember all the moving around and I can almost hear the sound of my dad swearing but I am grateful that they decided to move back to St. Anthony and not somewhere else.

The next eight years of my life are what I refer to as my "Wonder Years", because like the famous show, my life while growing up in St. Anthony was filled with many adventures where everyday something new and exciting was waiting to be discovered. These years were indeed the best years of my life.

Best of Friends
Chapter 3

I was five years old and ready to start kindergarten the year we arrived back in St. Anthony, NL. We moved into our new home on Gully Bank Road and I quickly made friends with the other kids on the street.

Our neighbours had a daughter my age and we instantly became buddies. She was friendly and curious, had orange hair and freckles, and talked with such a thick NL accent that I had trouble understanding her at first. She asked why my eyelashes were so long and told me I had the nicest blue eyes she had ever seen. I had a crush on her right away. It was the first of many crushes that I would have while growing up in St. Anthony.

I then met the boy two houses down from us and even though I did not know it at the time we would end up becoming best friends. His name was Dwayne and he was a grade ahead of me but when you are young and living in a small town age means nothing. He was only six at the time but looked older due to his dark complexion, jet-black hair and eyebrows, and what appeared to be the start of a moustache developing. I remember thinking to myself that I wished I had hair on my face like him, not knowing then what a pain in the ass it is to shave. We liked each other immediately and with the exception of being in different classes in school we became inseparable.

I often wished I had kept in touch more with Dwayne and many years ago I learned that his mother had passed away. She was one of the nicest ladies I knew and I would look forward to going to their house because she always had something homemade to offer me. Even if I had just ate I would always be polite and sit at the table while she proceeded to serve homemade pea soup, fresh bread, moose stew, salt beef, and many other delicacies that are considered staples of any NL family. She was a wonderful cook and while I ate I would pretend I could understand Dwayne's father while he talked to me but I have yet to meet anyone who talked as fast and with such a thick NL accent as Rod.

Many times he would finish what he was saying and then look to me for a reply but the fact was I had not understood one word of what he had said. I knew a nod of the head just would not suffice so the only logical thing to say was "Yes bye, you don't say?" as this response was very common in NL. This usually worked except when he asked me a question requiring a specific response, which unfortunately was often the case, and then everyone erupted into a fit of laughter because they knew I had not understood a word he said. Then Rod would say something like "Lard Jesis Ben bye, ya didn't understand one ting dat I sid, didya?" and Dwayne and I would start laughing so hard that I almost pissed myself on several occasions.

Dwayne and I were best buddies and when together our mischievous and adventurous nature was a force to be reckoned with. We took turns kissing all the girls in the neighbourhood; broke into and explored the abandoned houses on our street; built a tree house next to my house and smoked homemade cigars made of hemlock and sweet grass, just to name a few.

We were the kings of our neighbourhood and would defend it from anyone who did not live on Gully Bank Road. Defending usually meant a brutal snowball fight, a life or death wrestling match, or in extreme cases, throwing rocks at the intruders. Sorry Blair, I do not think Jeff really meant to hit you in the forehead, but it was a good throw!

Dwayne and I were both in karate for many years and often argued who was better than the other. He was older, bigger, had facial hair, and was probably stronger, though I would never admit it and would never back down from any challenge to a sparring match.

I always won more medals for the "kata" competitions, which is a series of techniques and karate moves combined together, and must be executed with speed, strength, agility, and precision. I am trying to make it sound cooler and more important than the "sparring" competitions that Dwayne would clean up in. That friggin' arsehole; he did not even know about the karate club until I told him about it. If I knew he was going to join I probably would not have told him and his older brother that I was already a black belt because when Dwayne joined and saw that the belt I was wearing was in fact a white belt him and his brother made fun of me for weeks.

His older brother Darryl would relentlessly tease me and say, "What color belt do you have now Ben, checkered?" Then they would start giggling. I felt like such a bull-shitter, which I was. But by the age of thirteen

Dwayne and I both had our brown belts and I think after I left St. Anthony he went on to become a black belt.

Dwayne, if you are reading this, thanks you for the good memories and for being a true friend. I have not had that feeling of true friendship for some time now and these days I need it more than ever. But I do not forget easily and what I remember of you is that you are a great person who I am grateful to have met. Please hear me when I say I am truly sorry for not staying in touch but I am not the same person I was when I was a kid. But then again, who is? Unfortunately, our life experiences play a huge role in who we become and mine have led me on a path of pain, anger, criminality, and a complete loss of identity. You knew me better than most people in my life now, and I will not lie to you. I have become an expert at burying my pain, my rage, and what I have been through. But I remember who I was. I was a funny, smart, strong, adventurous, and fearless boy that you had the pleasure of knowing. If you are reading this book please do not judge me on the mistakes I have made since I left St. Anthony, as they do not define the person I really am.

Who is Ben Cox?
Chapter 4

As I get older and watch my daughter grow up I cannot help but reminisce about my childhood experiences as they play a key role in how I view myself. For a while I lost all sense of myself but these days I am trying to reconnect with the boy that I left behind so many years ago.

The next chapter is dedicated to him in the hopes that I can reconnect with that adventurous, creative, strong, steadfast, and bravely wondrous kid I once was, that has been forgotten about for so long.

These are a few of his adventures while he lived on Gully Bank Road as well as stories from others who had the privilege to know him. He is greatly missed.

'Ben Dickey'

This is one of the earliest stories that my mother remembers and still often tells anyone willing to listen. It takes place the first year we moved to St. Anthony for the second time and I had just started kindergarten at my new school. Mom says there was one particular little girl who really liked me and went home after the first day of school and told her mother there was a boy in her class that is really cute. This little girl's mother knew Mom and I believe worked with her at the hospital.

*Anyway, when asked by her mother what my name was, the little girl looked down at her feet and said very shyly, "Well, his first name is Ben, but I can't tell you his last name because it's a really bad word". Her mother looked at her confused and asked, "What do you mean a bad word? It cannot be that bad if it's his last name. Just tell me what his last name is". The little girl then replied matter-of-factly "Well, I don't want to say it, but its kind-of the same as **Dickey**".*

Her mother knew right away that she was talking about Jane and Danny Cox's boy and later told my parents the story and they all roared with laughter.

So, to the little girl, you know who you are, I want to thank you for giving my parents a story that they never get tired of telling complete strangers or anyone sitting at the dinner table. I really enjoy hearing it over and over again. Awesome!

'Oh my God. He's Dead!'

I think every kid secretly fantasizes at some point about what people would say if they died or how upset their friends and family would be. I usually thought of this scenario after I had been punished or grounded and would imagine those who had wronged me crying and wishing they never yelled at me or spanked me when I was alive. Trust me, I know it sounds horrible, but I was not really going to kill myself.

Anyway, one night a bunch of us kids from the neighbourhood were playing and goofing around on one of the big snow banks that the storm had created the night before. Keep in mind that the snow banks in St. Anthony would often reach over ten feet high and those were just the drifts. The usual gang was there, including, Dwayne, Michelle, Renetta, and I.

As usual, Dwayne and I were tormenting the others to death, stopping every now and then to make out with them and then immediately go back to tormenting. Once we all became bored with this arrangement, we would trade partners. We were like one big happy family and this was an ordinary night on Gully Bank Road.

While the girls were busy gossiping about which boy kissed better (obviously it was me because Dwayne gave them what appeared to be carpet burns from his moustache!), I whispered to Dwayne "Watch this!" and I reached up and grabbed a telephone wire that was easily reachable from the top of the snow bank.

I knew I had to make it look good so I twisted and screamed and shook my body in such a way that it probably resembled someone having a grand mal seizure. I also made a low humming sound with my throat and after about fifteen seconds of this I let myself go completely limp and fell face first into the snow bank.

The scream that Michelle let out was something that I have yet to hear from another human being since and it did not help that Dwayne was playing along with it perfectly. Without as much as a grin he screamed "Oh shit, Ben, please oh God, please don't be dead, this isn't happening, Jesus Christ this can't be happening . . ."

I still did not move and by this time Michelle was crying into my jacket and begging me to hang on. Renetta had already started the descent down the snow bank and was screaming and sobbing for someone, anyone, to come and help. The sight of her sliding and sobbing simultaneously was too much for Dwayne to contain and he started giggling. With Dwayne and I, when one of us started giggling it was like a chain reaction and I immediately joined in with my own muffled giggling as my face was still buried in the snow.

Michelle is not stupid and most times a lot quicker than both of us so it did not take her long to figure out what was happening. She also had one hell of a temper and immediately started cursing *and pounding on us, yelling "You little sons of bitches. Ben, I honestly thought you were dead, and Dwayne you little frigger, you knew the whole time, didn't you?" We then realized Renetta had gone for help and was almost to Dwayne's house by the time we called her to come back.*

Believe me when I tell you that she also knew how to swear and when she was mad you had better watch out. By this time Dwayne and I had gone from giggling into those fits of laughter where you cannot catch your breath, all the muscles in your stomach ache, and you are very close to pissing your pants.

After about half an hour trying to calm them down and trying to stop laughing we went right back to where we left off, kissing the girls and packing snow down the backs of their necks. How I miss the good old days.

'Fire'

Like most boys, for Dwayne and I, the idea of having something we were not supposed to have was both frightening and exciting. We knew if we were caught our fathers would surely have skinned us like a couple of harp seals. Because we were very young at the time, the list of items that would fit into this category was quite extensive and included slingshots, knives, guns, porn movies, playboy magazines, cigarettes, alcohol, and in this case, lighters or matches.

Now Dwayne and I considered ourselves to be experts in most of these areas and we had lit many fires prior to today always extinguishing them once we felt they were getting out of control. However, on this particular day we were getting increasingly braver with each fire that we lit and would see how big we could let it get before putting it out.

We were in our usual fire starting location, which was on top of the hill behind Doug and Naomi Penny's house. This was a favourite spot of ours because we were out of view of any house and there was a natural rock fort there where we often brought girls so that there was no chance of their fathers ever catching us. It was autumn then and all the grass was dead and dry so starting a fire was very easy except for the strong wind that would make lighting the lighter difficult.

I cupped my hands around the lighter while Dwayne lit the grass and our teamwork paid off. We watched as the fire consumed a good portion of grass and when we were satisfied we both began to stamp it out with our feet. But the wind had picked up and as soon as we beat out one section the wind would cause another to become engulfed in flames. We took off our jean jackets and attempted with desperation to beat out the hot spots but it was no use. We could not control it. We both began to panic and knew that we had a big problem. We also knew we were in deep shit! Just as we were about to run for help we saw Doug Penny running toward us with a fire extinguisher. He had seen the smoke from his window and after about five minutes of continuous spraying from the fire extinguisher he had managed to put out the fire. As the three of us stood there and surveyed the damage I saw my dad coming toward us with the look of pure rage on his face. Dwayne had noticed him as well, and blurted out, "Oh shit!" and took off running leaving me standing there alone to face the wrath of God, otherwise known as my dad. I could feel my eyes beginning to fill up with tears and I am not sure if he saw the smoke or if Doug called him before he left but I remember saying to him, "Please don't kill me."

I think I have blocked from my memory what happened after that and in all honesty I would rather not try and recall it. What I do know is that I did not see Dwayne for at least a month after that except for when we sat on the bus together. Neither of us ever brought up again what happened that day.

'Who Wants to Build a Raft?'

While living in St. Anthony I made many good friends but there were two families who we spent a lot of time with. We were always getting together whether it was going over for supper, sleepovers, skiing trips to Marble Mountain, and many summer vacations.

They were our parent's best friends so that deemed us, as their children, to end up spending lots of time together. It also destined us boys (sorry Ellen and Laura) for great adventures. Between both families there are just too many stories that I could write about but, unfortunately, I had to narrow it down to one story but please know that I have equally fond memories of all of you.

This particular adventure involves, James and "Little" Ben, from the "H" family, and my brother Jeff and I ("Big" Ben). James' and "Little" Ben's sister, Ellen, also plays a role in this story and it is a perfect example of why we rarely included her in our more daring adventures. I think another one of our friends was there as well but for the life of me I cannot remember who he was. Sorry whoever you are.

Anyway, all four of us boys and Ellen, who we were told to watch out for, made our way along the shoreline to one of the government wharves that was nearby. It was during spring and all the ice was gone from the harbour. The tide was also low and had left behind piles of driftwood, various wooden pallets, rope, and other neat things that we took our time examining.

I blame what happened next on the movie I had watched several days ago, called "Huck", an adaption of the Tom Sawyer and Huckleberry Fin book. In the movie an orphan boy runs away and meets a slave who becomes his best friend. They both build a raft and float down the Mississippi River going from one great adventure to another. This movie and others such as

"The Goonies" and "Stand by Me" are made to bring out the adventurous spirit in every boy.

James and I being the oldest, and usually the masterminds of any new and daring schemes, came up with the idea of building a raft. It did not take long to convince our younger brothers that this was a brilliant idea. Ellen had now met a little girl her own age and was content to play with her so the four of us began the tedious construction of what we pictured would be the ultimate water vessel. "Little" Ben even mentioned building a cabin on it but James and I told him he was being ridiculous and if he wanted to be a part of the crew he had to follow our orders carefully. That kept him quiet for the time being.

Within a few hours we had what resembled a raft taking shape but without a hammer and nails and only rope to work with it was not the sturdiest of all vessels. We reinforced it with more rope, old tires on the bottom, and added more wooden pallets to the deck. When we were satisfied that it would hold all four of us we launched it into the water making sure to attach a rope from it to the shore so we could pull ourselves in when needed.

One by one the crew climbed aboard. First to board were James and I as we were the two captains and next to go was the first mate, my brother Jeff. Last but not least the greenhorn/deckhand, "Little" Ben, jumped aboard. I pushed us off with the long wooden pole we found and James held the rope that anchored us to shore. "It's really floating", cried "Little" Ben. "No duh, of course it floats" James replied with stern conviction as if the possibility that it would not float had never even crossed his mind. James and I looked at each other with the same expression of annoyance on our faces. Maybe taking on this young deckhand was not such a great idea after all. We ignored him and proudly stood on our raft and looked over the harbour that was now ours to explore. We let the rope go out further to where the water was black and the bottom was no longer visible. The long pole was of no use now but we were securely tied to a large rock on the shore and had plenty of rope yet to slack off and allow us to go out further. It was complete freedom.

We did this for some time, pulling the raft in then letting the tide carry us out until the rope was stretched to its full length. Suddenly, we noticed that Ellen had disappeared from where she had been playing and remembering that we were responsible to watch her we immediately began to panic and started to haul ourselves to shore. As we were drifting in we saw a little figure pointing at us from the top of the road. Then we recognized the two larger figures approaching with her and our panic levels went up a notch. Our mothers were sprinting toward us frantically shrieking and waving their arms in our direction. It would seem that while we had been distracted Ellen had snuck off to go tell our parents what the four of us were up to.

As both moms were very cautious women when it came to the safety of their kids, I guess it was understandable that they were quite upset. At the time though, we did not see what the big deal was, after all, we had built a very solid raft and had the foresight to attach an anchor to the shore. They should have appreciated our ingenuity if nothing else, right? Wrong!

The scolding continued as they marched us back home and the phrases, "No life jackets on . . ." and "You all could have drowned . . ." were repeated continuously. It was not until the phrase, "Just wait till your father comes home" that I really started to pay attention. Dad was especially famous for his temper and I, being the oldest, would surely bear the brunt of his anger when he got home.

The little girl ahead of us was now skipping along, repeating loudly, "You're in trouble, you're in trouble", and was completely oblivious to the four "death stares" that were focused on the back of her sweet little head.

'Papa, I Found Them!'

This next story is dedicated to my late grandfather, "Papa", as he always told it best. I was in grade four or five at the time, and my grandparents were visiting us from Harrington Harbour. I was on my way home on the school bus and was pretty excited to see "Mama and Papa", which all of us grandchildren called them.

We were discussing my day at school and laughing at Papa's stories when my father asked me, "Where are your glasses Ben?" Now, for those of you who do not know me I am infamous for misplacing my glasses and the reason for this was because I hated wearing them. I would always take them off my face and put them in my pocket so no one would see me with them on. Dad would get furious at me especially when my teachers would tell him they did not even know I wore glasses but had noticed me squinting a lot in class.

Anyway, I told Dad my glasses were in my pocket, and he smirked at Papa and said, "That's unusual, Ben, for your glasses to be in your pocket and not on your face!" This caused Papa to start grinning his famous grin. Dad told me to go get them and put them on but when I searched both pockets they were not in there. I thought to myself, "Oh shit, not again", made my way back into the kitchen and told Dad that I could not find them.

"Do not tell me you lost another pair, Lord Jesus Ben. Well when did you see them last?" I told him I put them in my pocket when I was waiting for the bus outside the school. So, off we went to look around the school parking lot and if they were not there we knew they had to be on the bus. We searched for some time before I finally found my glasses, though, I think it would have been better if I had never found them, period.

I had a habit of trying to make bad news sound good so when I walked into the kitchen I proudly stated, "Papa, Papa, I found my glasses!" He patted me on the back and said, "Did you my man, oh that's wonderful. Where did you find them?" I told him how we searched the whole parking lot and that I found them on the gravel area where the buses park. Then dad walked in behind me and asked me if I had shown Papa my glasses yet, which I had not done. I reached into my pocket and placed them on the table and Papa almost choked on his mouthful of beer.

They had been completely flattened! Both lenses were crushed and the ears were sprawled apart at a bizarre angle suggesting they had most likely been run over by one or all six of the buses that pulled out of the school parking lot. Then Papa said, "Well, at least you found them. That's the main thing." He grinned and winked at my father, who I could see, was not amused.

Why Me?
Chapter 5

It was 1994 and I was in grade seven, my last year of elementary school. I was a funny, outgoing, confident, and popular kid who got along with just about everyone. I had close friends, most of which I had known since kindergarten, and I was excited about starting high school with them. I loved the town of St. Anthony and knew it like the back of my hand. I had so many good memories and did not see coming what was about to happen next.

Jeff and I were upstairs reading Archie comics when Mom called us to come downstairs. She and Dad were sitting on the couch and told us they needed to talk to us about something. They told us they were unhappy and needed some time apart for a while. It did not feel real when they were telling me this and I guess I tried not to think about how my life was about to change.

I will not get into who wanted the separation or who said what to whom, because frankly, I did not give a shit. What mattered to me was moving out of the home we lived in for over eight years, having to have separate visits with Dad, and moving with mom to several different apartments around St. Anthony. I felt like I was the only one of my friends who had parents that were separated and I was embarrassed to tell anyone. I continued to hang on to the chance that they would get back together but as time went on I knew that would not be the case.

One night when we were sleeping at Dad's apartment he introduced us to a new female friend of his, who was a medical student from the United Kingdom (UK). I knew they were more than friends and as time went on the news kept getting worse, for Jeff and I anyway. Dad was planning to move to Britain with his lady friend and mom told us that she needed to move as well as she had decided to go back to university to get a degree in Nursing.

I was furious at them both; at Dad because I did not understand how he could leave his boys and move overseas with a woman he had known for less than a year. She did not know Dad like I did nor did she need him as badly as Jeff and I. I was also angry with Mom for making us move from a place I called home for as long as I could remember.

They gave Jeff and I the choice to go with either of them but I did not want to live anywhere except St. Anthony. It was the hardest choice I ever had to make, as I loved both my parents very much. We decided to stay with Mom because at least Dad had someone with him.

Before we left my friends threw a going away party for me at Heather's house and I said my final goodbyes to those who knew me so well. I knew that I would miss them when I left and I was terrified to be moving somewhere new but I pretended to be strong and in control. I was neither.

The next day we left St. Anthony and began the long drive to Hamilton, ON, which to me was the same as moving to Pakistan. I sat in the back seat and stared out the window most of the way because I did not want mom or Jeff seeing how much I was hurting or how much I missed Dad. I knew my eyes would give away too much so I kept facing the window and we continued to drive further away from the place and the people that I knew and loved.

•

*"I used to be a little boy, so old in my shoes . . . and what
I choose is my choice, what's a boy supposed to do?"*

—*Smashing pumpkins*

The New Kid (Twice)
Chapter 6

Being the new kid sucks! We had gotten settled into our
shitty apartment in Dundas, ON, which is a town located
just minutes from the city of Hamilton. I remember being
very nervous on my first day of grade eight, which is still
middle school in ON. The school was huge and packed
with strange faces and I felt completely alone. I thought
about my friends and how I wished I could be sitting
with them in what would have been my first year of high
school.

I was late for my first class because I could not find it
and when I walked in everyone was already sitting down. I
could feel everyone looking at me and whispering amongst
themselves. Two boys in the class were looking at me and
laughing, and if I were back in St. Anthony, I would have
said, "What the hell are you two dick-heads giggling at?"

But I was not in St. Anthony, not even in Newfoundland anymore, so I kept to myself and continued to observe my surroundings. I began to realize how different I was from the other kids. My thick Newfoundland accent caused everyone to snicker whenever I spoke and the clothes that I chose to wear my first day looked nothing like what the other kids were wearing.

The "Skaters" all wore baggy t-shirts, baggy jeans, and Airwalk sneakers. The "Rappers" wore XXL jeans from Stiches and pulled them down to their knees causing them to resemble a penguin when they walked. The "Stoners" wore shirts with "Nirvana" or "Pearl Jam" on them, their pants were corduroy bell-bottoms (which I did not know existed anymore) and they always played "hacky-sack" at recess and lunch break. Then there were the "Jocks", who usually had a Michigan State, Notre Dame, or Georgetown jacket on.

But where did I fit in? I did not consider myself as belonging to any of those groups and each of my friends back home were unique to themselves. None of us had ever belonged to a certain category. We either liked one another or we did not, simple as that. But at that age nothing was more important to me than fitting in. The need to have an identity or to "belong" is one of the most important things in every teenager's life, and I was no different. I also soon found out that I was very adaptable and with time everything got easier.

I still missed Dad a lot and many nights when I was alone in my room I would cry long and hard into the pillow. It was not because I was sad or scared, I was just hurt and there was so much anger inside me that sometimes I could not hold it in. I know sometimes Mom and my brother felt like they were walking on eggshells because it did not take much for me to lose it.

By the time I finished grade 8 I was no longer thought of as the new kid. I had made many good friends from my class, knew my way around town, and had a busy social life. My grades had dropped but I did not care because all I cared about was finally feeling like I fit in.

I spent the summer hanging out with my best friends and getting into a little trouble but nothing too serious (although my mother may disagree). My pastimes included swimming at the lake, rollerblading, smoking weed, playing basketball, and chasing girls.

When my friends and I started our first year of high school we thought we were the shit. We were getting noticed by older girls, getting high with older boys, and skipping class to go hang out in the city. The movie "Dazed and Confused" had just come out and it was an immediate hit with every teenager. It even portrayed how our first day of school went, as some of us were paddled, a few taped to trees, and others, like me, were forced to ask senior girls if they would marry us. But later in the year when no one was looking the same girls would give me their phone numbers and tell me to call them. Thanks Christy and Carrie. Our lives revolved around hanging out with our friends, trying to have sex, smoking weed, drinking beer, skipping class, playing ball, and harassing the two Asian owners of the Dundas Pizzeria where we all hung out.

The only drugs that I had tried up to this point were marijuana and sometimes hash oil when it was around. Then, one day during lunchtime, my best friend BJ asked me if I wanted to try Acid. I said "Fuck that man, I got math class after lunch." But he was very persistent and said he would skip with me and stay with me in case I tripped out.

Of course with me being easily influenced and always willing to try new things, I finally agreed to try it. He gave me the small piece of paper and told me to put it under my tongue, which I did. Then I asked him if he was going to take his, to which he replied, "I only bought one and I wanted you to tell me what it feels like before I try it".

What a dick! I made him swear not to leave my side, as I did not know what to expect. The bell rang indicating lunch break was over and we headed to the far end of the park so we were out of view from the school.

What seemed like hours went by as I waited for something to happen. I said, "Someone ripped you off bro, because I don't feel a damn thing". Ten minutes later it hit me square between the eyes and I felt like I was in a dream world where I was walking and talking but felt as though nothing was real. And then the paranoia hit me. I yelled, "Holy shit man, I am really fucked up. This isn't even funny." BJ was now laughing his ass off and waving his hands in my face saying, "You're tripping out dude, whoa, what's that on your face, what the hell is that?" I told him I had to sit down, so we sat in the grass and I just stared at the blue sky and told him to keep talking to me.

We shared a few joints and smoked about a pack of cigarettes between the two of us. Hours passed by like minutes and soon the bell rang letting us know we could go and find the rest of our friends who knew I took the acid and were curious to know what it felt like.

As we were about to head back to school and mix in with the crowd coming out I noticed my mother's car drive right past us and turn into the school. I turned as white as a ghost and BJ asked me, "What's your mom doing here?" It was then I remembered why she was here today. I had completely forgotten that she was going to pick me up after school for a dentist appointment in the city. BJ burst into a fit of laughter and I yelled, "It's not funny you dick, I can't get in that car like this, I feel like I'm dreaming man! What do I do?"

BJ, who was thinking clearly, said, "You have to go with her, or she'll go into the school looking for you and find out that you skipped class, dummy". He was right so I told myself, "Pull it together, Ben, you can do this, just remember this is reality and you have to act normal".

BJ wished me luck as I walked away from him and got in the front passenger seat of Mom's car. "How was school today?" she asked me, to which I replied, "It was alright". As we drove off I saw BJ in the side mirror surrounded by a crowd of our friends who were all listening to him as he was laughing and pointing in the direction of Mom's car. He really was a dick!

I managed to somehow hold it together the rest of the day which included not freaking out at the stool in the dentist's office that appeared to be moving on its own, or at my brother who I thought was staring at me the entire time we were eating supper.

The effects of the LSD lasted approximately fourteen hours and after a sleepless night and vowing never to do it again I made my way to school where BJ and the rest of our friends were anxiously waiting for me in our usual smoking hangout. BJ was the first to speak, asking me "So, how did your dentist appointment go?" To which I replied, "Just give me a smoke, asshole!"

My main group of friends consisted of Jeff, Tanya, Carrie, Tony, and last but not least, BJ, who was my best friend. Later that year he moved with his mom to Hamilton and I used to travel by bus every weekend to go visit him. I used to love going over to his place because I thought his mom was the coolest mother ever and we never had to hide anything from her.

His older brother also came to live with them to go back to high school to get his diploma. Both BJ and I thought of his brother as our hero and we wanted to be just like him when we got older. He always had a beautiful girl over and nobody would ever mess with us when he was around. He had recently just got out of prison before moving in with BJ and was as tough as they come but he was always nice to us.

Mom, however, hated me going over there because she thought BJ was a bad influence on me and she may have been right. But he was my best friend and back then I did not care what she thought. Like most teenagers I was very rebellious and school and family usually were a distant second in my priorities. I just wanted to have fun. So that is what I did.

By the end of the school year three of my closest friends knew they were not going to pass grade nine, and as for me, I was "placed ahead" with a 48 average, and an absenteeism record of nearly 35%. Mom was not pleased and I do not blame her. I was not the same boy I was when I left St. Anthony and she realized my downward spiral would continue if she stayed here another year. But much like St. Anthony we will never know what would have happened if I had stayed. And for the second time in three years I would again move from a place I had called my home.

"Have you gone psycho? I can't do this again mom; do you understand me? What was the point of the past two years trying to fit in and make new friends if we're just going to move again? Do you understand how hard it was on us when we left St. Anthony? Do you? I don't think you realize what you will be doing to me if I have to do this all over again. Look at me and hear me, please! You have to believe me when I tell you, I can't fucking do this again!"

I was furious with her and could not believe she was moving us again. Do not get me wrong; this is just how I felt during that time. I know now that she had to move for work. She had finished her two-year upgrade program and graduated from McMaster University with a degree in Nursing. She had been offered a job in Cape Breton, NS, and had accepted the offer.

I know she was doing it to support us but back then I did not and could not justify another move. I had a life there now, and was finally happy again. I continued to try and persuade her to let me stay with one of my friends and promised I would study and keep my grades up in grade ten. I promised to quit smoking weed and to be respectful of her and nicer to my brother. I pretty much promised her everything but my soul, and I meant every word. I would give it all up if she would just let me stay in a place that I felt comfortable living in. The thought of starting in another school and trying to fit in again made me feel sick to my stomach. But her mind was made up and nothing I said could change that. I hated my mother at that moment and that hatred stayed with me for those remaining weeks in ON. And it only got worse when we moved to Cape Breton.

The year I lived in Cape Breton was one I would rather forget entirely. I usually do not even mention that I lived there for a year because in my mind it was a year that I should have spent in ON being happy. But I was there, they were my experiences, and I remember everything.

Before we moved to Cape Breton, I spent the summer crab fishing with my uncles and cousin in Harrington Harbour. I knew that we would be moving when I returned from fishing so I made sure I enjoyed my time in Harrington. It was one of the best summers of my life.

My aunt's new boyfriend met me at the airport and was going back to Harrington to see her. I had not met him before and Mom had mentioned he was deaf but could read lips very well and for the most part I understood everything he was trying to say to me. I remember him being very animated and excitable and always had a big grin on his face. I liked him immediately. I liked him even more when he asked me if I "toked", and he made a sucking sound with his fingers in front of his lips. While nodding my head I exclaimed, "Why yes, as a matter of fact I do!" With that his smile got much bigger. He then proceeded to root through his luggage until he pulled out a pair of loafers and from inside them he produced a "brick" of marijuana. At that moment I really liked my new uncle.

There is something inside me that changes when I visit Harrington Harbour and it is something I can both physically and mentally feel. Maybe it is my subconscious telling me that this is where I belong, and always have.

The smell of the sea and the aroma of fresh baked bread when I walk into Mama's house immediately sent signals to my brain that I was content. It seems natural to see Jeremy and Jessica, Uncle Randy, Aunt Madeleine, Uncle Harry, Aunt Kimberly, and Mama and Papa, as if I have lived here my entire life. There is no amount of therapy greater than stepping off the ferry in Harrington Harbour and knowing you are back where your father grew up and where you are among family.

I spent the majority of the summer hanging out with Jeremy, my first cousin, who I have always felt close with. He is the biggest torment I have ever known and I had to stay sharp when working with him on his father's boat. I remember one early morning when we left to go fishing and Jeremy and I crawled in the cabin bunks, as was our usual routine. We were hungover from the night before and needed those extra hours of sleep before we began hauling up the crab pots and sorting the crab out. Jeremy was joking around and pretending to be a rapper in his oversized fishing gear but I was completely exhausted from the previous night and all I could do was yawn in response to his antics. Jeremy, being who he was, waited patiently and the next time I yawned he quickly shoved a piece of bait in my mouth, which happened to be a whole mackerel. I started cursing and spitting and Jeremy could not stop laughing. Once my uncles found out what had happened the whole crew were in tears from laughing so hard.

I would love to keep talking about that summer in Harrington but that would entail at least another two chapters, so I had better just move on.

Once we had obtained our quota of snow crab, the fishing season, for me anyway, was coming to an end. I had managed to save a considerable amount of money and will be forever grateful to my uncles who gave me a chance to work for them. I hope I did not slow them down too much.

I flew back to ON and was only there for a few days before we began our journey to Cape Breton. I immediately recognized the town of Ingonish, Cape Breton, as we had vacationed there numerous times from NL when I was younger. However, moving there and vacationing there were two completely different things, which I would soon come to find out.

It did not take me long to fit in. I had started talking to a few guys at the bus stop on my first day of school and mentioned that I was looking to buy some weed. They all referred me to two guys that lived at the top of the hill. These two guys were older than me and had dropped out of school. I was introduced to them when I got off the bus after school that day and from that day forward the three of us were inseparable. We did not have much in common except that we all liked to get high. They loved having me around because I always had money to buy drugs and within a few months I managed to spend every cent of money that I had saved from crab fishing the summer before. The only thing I cared about was smoking dope and when my money ran out I started stealing from my mom.

I hated this small town and the school I was in. I missed the freedom of the city and all my friends in ON. I missed playing basketball in the park and rollerblading everywhere I went. I still missed Dad too who I had not seen now for over two years. As time went on I started to care less and less about school, family, or the consequences of my actions. Within the span of nine months I had become someone that I did not even recognize in the mirror.

Mom could not control me and did not know what to do to help me. By the end of the school year I had a criminal record, numerous breaches of probation, was suspended from school for fighting, used drugs daily and drank heavily every weekend, had my nose crushed by one of the toughest guys in Ingonish, messed around with my best friend's girlfriend, missed all my final exams because I was in a Juvenile Correctional Facility in Waterville, NS, and ended up failing grade ten.

Near the end of that school year Mom and I had a huge argument because she would not let me hitchhike to the town where my girlfriend lived and I was so angry with her I put my fist through the bathroom door. She got scared and called the RCMP to come pick me up and they charged me with a breach of probation and damage to property. She refused to let me back into the house with her so I was taken to a holding cell until my court date.

Mom and the Constable were in the front of the police car and I was in the back cursing, screaming, and beating on the glass the whole way to the holding cell. Mom tried to hug me and tell me she loved me as I was being taken inside but I told her to get the fuck away from me and that I never wanted to see her face again. That was the last time I spoke to her for over a year.

Second Chance
Chapter 7

I could not believe how much my life had changed in the three years since my parents divorced and I left St. Anthony. Here I was sitting in a holding cell waiting to go back to the Correctional Centre and this time for a much longer period of time. I could not believe Mom had called the cops and had me arrested and I felt so betrayed by her that I did not care if I never saw her again. I really felt completely and hopelessly alone at that point. I had stopped caring about my family and myself and I just wanted to end it.

After about a week in cells I was brought to the courthouse and was prepared to go back in custody at Waterville. What I was not prepared for was seeing my dad and his girlfriend, Kara, in the courtroom. I guess Mom must have called them and let them know what was happening. They had returned from the UK and were now living in Roddickton, NL, not far from St. Anthony where I grew up.

I really was not expecting what happened next. When the judge asked if any of my parents were present in the courtroom Dad stood up, approached the judge, and told him that he and my stepmom were prepared to take me with them to NL. He explained that I had moved around several times in the past three years and that it had been hard on me with him being gone for so long. He told the judge, "Ben needs his father, and he is coming with me".

The judge agreed to this but told me I needed to take full advantage of this second chance I have been given because there would not be another one. He ordered me to be on probation for another year and then said I was free to leave with Dad and stepmom.

Outside the courthouse Dad, my stepmom, and Mom were waiting for me and I did not realize how much I missed him until he hugged me and I could not stop from crying into his shoulder. I wanted to prove to him that I had the potential to do something good with my life and I knew that I wanted to make him proud of me.

As we were driving to Sydney to catch the ferry to NL they told me they had some news. Kara was pregnant and I was going to have not one but two sisters as they had just found out she was carrying twins. "Holy shit, congratulations", I said.

Dad proceeded to lecture us on how potent his sperm still was and that Kara did not stand a chance against his seed. I started laughing and told him that was the most disturbing thing I had ever heard and so the dirty jokes and the laughs continued as we made our way to Roddickton, NL.

It had been three years since I had to leave that province that I loved so much and here I was now finally going back. I was also very happy to be with Dad again. I had a clean slate when I moved back and I had forgotten how friendly and welcoming the people there were. No one knew anything from my past unless I told them and I was simply recognized as the doctor's son. It was good to spend time with Dad again and get back to the things we used to enjoy doing when I was younger. We went snowmobiling, ice fishing, hunting, and I gradually started to feel more like the person I was before I left St. Anthony.

We eventually moved into a larger house because Kara was close to having the twins and we would need the extra space when they arrived. I became close friends with the guys around my street and they were a good influence on me throughout my stay in Roddickton. Dad bought me my very own snowmobile and I drove that thing every winter even driving it to school every day like most of the other kids did.

Kara went into premature labour and her and Dad had to go to St. Johns, the capital city of NL, due to the complications that could arise from the premature delivery of twins.

Savannah was the smallest and weighed less than three pounds while Sadie was receiving more nutrients and weighed about five pounds. They were both beautiful little babies and had curly blond hair and bright blue eyes.

There was never a dull moment around the house when the twins were brought home and I still have the Barney songs stuck in my head, which were played around the clock. But it was a hell of a lot better than the Teletubbies, which was one of their favourite shows as they got older and made me feel like I was tripping out on LSD again.

I cannot pretend that I was completely reformed and that I never made any mistakes while living in Roddickton because that would simply be a lie. I had some bad habits that I found hard to let go of with the drug use being the worse one. I also stole money from Dad and Kara on several different occasions.

I do not know why they put up with me but I am very grateful that they did not give up on me during this time. I think they saw that I had potential to be good and hoped that I would start to grow up at some point. Though I was far from perfect I had calmed down quite a bit compared to what I was like in Cape Breton. Also, the friends I hung out with were far from criminals and though we did our fair share of partying they were all good guys at heart. So, Terry, Jerome, Willis, Gus, "Worm", Farrin, and Russell, I hope you are all doing well and I am sorry for not keeping in touch more but thank you all for the good memories and I feel privileged to have been able to call you my friends.

Yes, even Terry, despite the fact that he was one of the biggest torments I had ever met. Dad and I have oftentimes talked about some of the pranks he used to pull. Especially the time he was hiding outside the basement door waiting to scare the shit out of me when I came out. However, Dad came out first with his axe in his hand as he was going to chop some splits for the fireplace.

Thinking it was me, Terry grabbed Dad from behind and screamed, "YOU'RE DEAD!" in a deep voice. When he spun around with the axe raised Terry's eyes opened as wide as saucers and he made a high pitch squealing noise with his throat. Once Dad recognized who his attacker was he was furious and started cursing at Terry, "Don`t you ever try that again you little prick, I almost split your friggin forehead wide open. If you ever sneak up on me like that again, I`ll put this god damn axe right between your beady little eyes, do you understand me?"

I think Terry was in shock, and said something like "Jeez, I didn't think it was that bad, I was only having a laugh. I thought you were Ben." When I went outside Terry had already gone home. Dad explained that he would probably not be back anytime soon because he came very close to being murdered. Then he told me what happened and I could not stop laughing. I could tell by Dad`s expression, however, that he really got a scare, not so much by Terry grabbing him as by the fact that he came close to killing him. He told me later that he felt bad about yelling at Terry but I do not think he realized how close Dad was to bringing that axe down.

I messed around with many girls in high school but there was one in particular that I became very close with and loved very much. I will not mention her name but she knows who she is. We went out for about two years and spent every day together, usually hanging out upstairs in her grandparent's house. I know her grandparents did not like me too much because I was there every day and they thought we spent too much time together and not enough time with our friends and family. And they were right. Our lives revolved around each other and I really feel as though I ignored many of my close friends during that period. I hope they forgave me but I will admit that I was addicted to her and I loved every minute of it. Even Dad wondered if I still lived at their house because sometimes he would not lay eyes on me for weeks.

I need to try and describe our relationship without embarrassing her in the process so here it goes. For me it was an initial physical attraction that I had never felt before and she began to replace every bad habit I had in my life. I needed nothing else but to love her and know that she loved me. It has to be the same for most young adults but to me it was something special between us and nothing else mattered except when she was in my arms. It sounds romantic; however, at times it was anything but that. What we had was raw, euphoric, painful, obsessive, mentally and emotionally exhausting, uncensored, and unbridled. If I had to compare our relationship to anything it would have to be Rihanna`s music video, We Found Love, minus the raves, the hallucinogenic drugs, and him forcing her to get a tattoo on her ass.

One of us did give the other a tattoo though except I forced her into cutting her initial into me with a razor blade. Yeah, I know, we were crazy. Every time I look at the three prominent white scars in my shoulder I am reminded of the young and stupid boy that I was then. It is even more embarrassing when my eight year old daughter asks me, "Dad, why is there a big 'K' on your arm?" to which I reply, "I was born with it." Then I would get the stink eye from my wife at the time that hated the fact that there was a constant reminder of an ex-girlfriend permanently engraved into my shoulder. I really have to get this thing covered over or else start looking for a girl with the first initial "K" in her name.

During my last year of high school Dad informed me about a job at the nursing home where they needed someone to help out bathing the elderly male residents. The man that had been doing the job for years had quit due to back problems as there were no Hoyer lifts there and you basically had to lift the men from the wheelchair into the old fashioned tub. Once they were bathed they had to be lifted out and dried off and once back in their rooms they were dressed, shaved, combed, and wheeled down to the dining room for lunch. The job was hard but also extremely rewarding.

Dad, who is a registered nurse, knew it would be awkward for me at first so on my first day he accompanied me and showed me the basics in caregiving. He also showed me how to properly lift with my legs so I would not hurt my back. I knew that if he could do it then maybe I could as well.

With time I got used to what I was doing and realized that we all get old and eventually would need help as these residents did. It also felt good to help them and they could see that I was not embarrassed or uncomfortable which seemed to put them at ease. Dad and Kara were also very impressed with me and told me they never would have thought that I would be comfortable doing that type of work. For the first time in a while I felt proud of myself and I know Dad was proud of me as well.

I continued caring for the residents at the nursing home for almost my entire last year of high school and after many chats with Dad about what I wanted to do when I graduated, I decided to follow in my parent's footsteps and try nursing as a career. I worked extra hard in my last year of high school and graduated with a very good average. That combined with the experience I had from my job at the nursing home was enough to get me accepted into the Bachelor of Science (Nursing) program at St. Francis Xavier University (STFX) in Antigonish, NS.

University? Me?
Chapter 8

I left for university in 2000 and I remember being both nervous and excited about starting the nursing program. I had heard from others how difficult it was and I was dreading biochemistry as chemistry was one of my worse subjects in high school. Even my girlfriend at the time had tried out nursing school in NL the year before but lost interest in it after the first semester. She was much smarter than me when it came to school so of course I was worried about how I would adapt to the workload.

In my first semester I lived in the infamous Burke House, which had a reputation on campus as being the rowdiest, loudest, and most unruly dorm at STFX. It was famous for its annual hockey game with our rival Mac House and the ensuing chaos that accompanied it known simply as Bur-Mac. Bur-Mac started as a friendly game between two all-male houses and for many years it had never been a problem. Both houses kept it friendly and it culminated over a game of hockey. Then the parties would commence. The rival houses started pranking one another and the usual problems of property destruction, excessive drinking, and fighting soon followed in Bur-Mac's wake. It was even mentioned by David Letterman when he named the event the second largest party in North America, second only to Mardi Gras. The year I lived there was the last year Burke was an all-male house and I was one of the many guys that were told we had to find somewhere else to live the following semester.

STFX wanted to make Burke co-ed and start fresh with a new group of first year students. There was just too much vandalism, fighting, drinking, partying, dropouts and expulsions coming from this dorm on campus. I watched several of my good friends dropout and one of my buddies got expelled for breaking another guy's jaw.

When we returned the following semester everyone was scattered throughout campus as well as off-campus and though we tried to reenact those days when we lived in Burke it just was not the same anymore. Most of us, me included, were on the verge of flunking the majority of our first year courses. We had all gained about fifteen or so pounds (known as the freshman fifteen) from months of excessive drinking and ordering from The Wheel Pizzeria. I had cracked three of my front teeth from diving head first into a dunk tank during Frosh week initiations, an event I only vaguely recollect. I could not remember the faces or names of a lot of the girls I slept with during that first semester and would frequently find myself getting glared at by girls who I could not recall seeing before.

Considering all this, I decided to take Mom up on her offer to stay with her. She had taken a job at STFX University as a Professor of Nursing and was renting a cottage on the outskirts of town. I thought this was a good idea because I had to start applying myself if I wanted to move on to my second year of nursing and this would be a quiet place to focus on my studies. By this time my girlfriend back in NL had grown sick of my bullshit and infidelities and she moved back to Alberta (AB), Canada, to be closer to her parents.

Mom and I were getting along pretty good and I told her how much I regretted all the heartache I put her through when I last lived with her four years ago. I could understand why she made the choices she did, and I knew she was doing the best she could to raise two boys as a single mother. And believe me Jeff and I were a handful and in many ways still are.

By the end of my first year of university I had passed every course except biochemistry; it certainly did not help that my attendance for lectures was only 60%. My second and third years were better and I was doing more clinical rotations and learning more about the skill components to nursing. I was discovering that I enjoyed the practical aspect of it and felt I had made a good choice to take nursing as a career. I struggled with a few of the harder science courses like anatomy and physiology and ended up having to repeat it to get the credits. However, in the nursing courses and the clinical rotations I proved I could hold my own.

I took a job at the nursing home in Antigonish and worked as a Primary Care Worker during the summer months in between school. I enjoyed my job there and getting to know patients and their families and assisting with their personal needs. Making them feel comfortable when providing care had always been one of my strongpoints. I often still think about the staff and the residents that I came to know so well there.

In my third year of university I met a girl by the name of Rachelle from one of my classes and we dated for several months. Later that year she decided to leave the nursing program and was planning to go back to her job as a Licensed Practical Nurse in AB. Both of us knew we were not in love so ending the relationship seemed like the best option at the time. She left for AB and I had come to terms that this was the right thing to do and I think she felt the same.

About a week later I got a call from Rachelle telling me we needed to talk. When her words "I`m pregnant" came to me over a long distance telephone call I felt sick to my stomach. I could not grasp that this was happening and all I could think of was how unprepared I was to become a father. This should be the happiest moment in any parent's life but the only emotions I felt were anger, fear, and panic. Now the guilt and shame start to gnaw at me as I recall the horrible things I said to her when I found out she would not even consider talking about any other options other than raising this baby. She had strong religious beliefs and I am usually pretty open and understanding to other people's moral and ethical values but this was not Ethics 101, this was my life we were talking about here. I could not understand for the life of me then why she wanted to have this baby when the two people involved were not in love or even together anymore. After many emotional arguments and verbal onslaughts from me she had made up her mind and the decision was final. Largely due to her beliefs, as well as a mother-baby connection that I could not have understood, she decided she would go ahead with the pregnancy. Eventually she returned to NS to be closer to her family and insisted on making a life for her and our baby with or without me.

I am not proud of myself for the thoughts and words that poured from my mouth over those nine months but I was proud on January 22, 2004, the day my little girl was born. I was there for the entire C-section as her mother was not dilating fully so the baby had to be delivered via surgery. She was so beautiful; blond haired with bright blue eyes and a reminder of all things good in me and in the world.

I know now that if her mother had listened to me I would never have been able to hold her or hear her call me Dad. I would never have known that her favorite meal is ribs and corn on the cob and I would never have snuggled with her in our bed when she was scared, which was most nights. I would never have watched her open her Christmas presents or had the privilege of kissing her sweet face and telling her how much I love her. And I will never forgive myself for initially not wanting her to be born.

Rachelle eventually met someone else who was actually a close friend of one of my roommates at the time. He is a great guy and I knew he cared a lot about my daughter. He was there for her since she was a baby and in many ways was more of a father to her than I ever was. I was not upset at all when they started going out as I was also dating someone at the time. But as my daughter got older she started calling him Dad as well which I knew was normal for any toddler who had a man living with her full-time.

I have come to accept it now since they have been together for eight years. As for my daughter, she essentially had two sets of parents that loved her equally and for the most part we all continued to stay civil with each other. I know Macy was happier because of this and for that I am grateful.

I have to admit though that I hated Rachelle back then for allowing my daughter to continue calling another man her dad. I often thought she was encouraging it because of the hurtful things I said to her in the past and this was her way to get back at me. I felt sick to my stomach when she referred to him as Dad, and once tried to explain to her the difference in a biological father and a stepfather. I could tell she did not understand though and I did not want to confuse her any more than she already was. When Rachelle caught wind of it she lectured me on the fact that her other dad spent more time with her than I ever did. And that is absolutely true. Also true, is that I only have joint custody and she is the main guardian, therefore if he lives with her then obviously he will spend the majority of the time raising her.

Rachelle would argue that I could have seen Macy more or phoned her more if I wanted to. And again, that is absolutely true. But I did not want to because I hated going over there and seeing my baby in his arms and then watching her kiss him goodbye and saying "I love you, Dad". I have never felt a more hurtful, painful, inadequate feeling as when my own flesh and blood spoke those words and I really do not think anything could make me feel worse. But I kept my mouth shut and buried that anger deep as I have done with many things that have hurt me throughout my life.

It was around this time that I once again started to feel unhappy with my life and myself. As I tried to ignore this feeling I was unknowingly putting myself on a path that would lead to the loss of my career, my marriage, my freedom, my sobriety, and worst of all, my self-worth.

I was in my final year of nursing and it was by far the most difficult year for me. I struggled to maintain a balance between classes, care plans, clinical, and fatherhood. I rarely saw my daughter and when I did take Macy for overnight it was in a house with three other roommates. Her mother usually provided me with enough supplies such as diapers and formula during those brief visits. I was in school full-time and only worked in the summer months at the nursing home. The only money I gave her in that first year was when I worked in the summer and the little I had left from my student loans during the school year as I was still paying my own tuition and rent. They also lived forty minutes away and I had no car at the time. I knew that eventually graduation would come and once I started my career I would be able to provide a much more stable means of child support. But it still did not make me feel anymore adequate as a father or as a man during Macy`s first year of infancy.

But I had Lyndsay. We were in nursing together and had hooked up several times after my ex, Rachelle, had left for AB. She knew I was going to be a father but that did not bother her at all. We stopped seeing each other for a while because I was pretty messed up at the time and did not want a relationship then. But shortly after Macy was born we met again at the nursing home during the summer and just started right where we left off. We continued to spend more and more time together and Macy and Lyndsay seemed to form a strong bond together. To this day she still calls her "Mommy Lyndsay", which she has done since she was a toddler.

I was so relieved to have someone to help me and confide in through those times that I ignored the thought that maybe I was feeling strongly toward her for the wrong reasons. I asked myself many times if this was fair to her or if I being honest with myself. Deep in my heart I think I knew the truth but somewhere along this path I began to alter my true thoughts and ignore the lessons and advice I received from my parents as a child. To quote my mother, "Follow your heart and stay true to who you are because life is too precious to waste it struggling with yourself." But it was hard being alone and I think I was really scared back then. Slowly I began to ignore all my instincts and what my self-conscience was telling me and instead opt for the path that was easiest both emotionally and financially.

Why not move in together and have two incomes to work with instead of one? I knew that I was graduating soon and I with that would come child support payments, student loan payments, rent, car payments, bills, credit card debt, and the list goes on. The more I thought of these new responsibilities which I had the luxury of not having as a student, the deeper my true feelings were buried. I simply started pretending I was content with my life but inside me I was screaming at myself, "Wake up, for god sake, snap out of it! You have never settled for anything in your life, so why start now? You cannot sacrifice happiness for convenience." But that is exactly what I did and what is worse is that I chose to do it. What the hell is wrong with me?

The Nurse
Chapter 9

I cannot believe I did it. I am really graduating from university. It was official now that all the hard work, the studying, cramming the night before exams, dragging myself to lectures hungover, and countless hours spent training during clinical rotations had finally paid off. Five years later and forty-five thousand dollars poorer here I was about to graduate with a Bachelor of Science degree in Nursing.

Nine years ago I was standing in front of a judge facing the return to the Correctional Centre for the second time in my life. Now, here I was shaking hands with the faculty of a university and being handed my degree by the Dean of Science. It was a proud day for me and I was glad to have my family there to share it with me.

Once I got the news that I passed my RN exams, which are separate from the actual degree program, I accepted a full time position as a float nurse at the Aberdeen Hospital, which is where Macy was born. It was a forty-minute commute from where our apartment was but they offered a sign on bonus of four thousand dollars, which I used to put toward a second hand car. Lyndsay was still finishing up her last year of nursing so we rented an apartment close to the university.

I was very nervous to be working on my own but the orientations I was given to each floor were excellent and with time my confidence in my practice and skills increased. If we did not know something we were made to feel comfortable in asking someone for advice and we were supervised closely until the more experienced nurses deemed us ready to take over our own patient loads.

I started on several medicine floors until I was able to gain experience in basic skills such as catheter and nasogastric tube insertions, dressing changes, IV insertions, maintenance of the IV pumps, physical assessments and medication administration. There was also the continuous charting and reporting on each patient and we had to learn time management skills or else we would quickly become overwhelmed.

After about two months there I was moved to the Surgery floor, which involved preparing patients for the operating room, taking care of post-operative patients recovering from a wide variety of surgeries, and dealing with the many complications that can arise after surgery, such as bleeds, infections, blood clots, pneumonia, and pain control. There was also an Orthopedic Unit which we took turns rotating on as the patients there were much heavier due to the nature of their surgeries. Most were on strict weight bearing restrictions and mobility was significantly decreased after surgery especially if they had a hip or knee replacement. I was definitely learning lots by this time and I was already being scheduled for shifts on both floors and over the next few months I worked mainly between the Surgery and Medicine Units.

My manager who wanted to know how I felt about spending the day in ER (Emergency Room) approached me one day. There was an overflow of patients there and the nurses were swamped. She said my supervisors and coworkers had good things to say about me and that I was a very hard working and capable nurse. I told her that I had never been orientated in the ER but she assured me I would only be an extra set of hands so downstairs and through the ER doors I went and she was right, the place was a gong show.

Two ambulances had arrived in the span of a half hour, which normally would not be uncommon, however both patients were immediately triaged as level ones, which means they are most likely critical, and need immediate attention. Everything else in the ER then gets put on hold and unless you are bleeding out, having a heart attack, or have stopped breathing, you quite simply have to wait until those critical patients have been stabilized.

I introduced myself to one of the nurses at the desk and asked if there was anything I could help with. She pointed at the stack of charts, took a deep breath, and without pausing said, *"They all need their vitals rechecked, several of them have IV meds past due, they are all ringing for something for pain, if they need to use the bathroom make sure they don't pull their IV lines out when they get up, the patient in the isolation room was just ordered IV antibiotics and needs an IV started in her left arm because she had a mastectomy on her right breast so you have to use her left arm and, once you get the IV in and the antibiotics going she needs to have her pre-op checklist done because she is going for surgery any minute now. Just remember to write down all the vitals here and don't forget to chart what medications you give on this sheet. Here are the keys to the narcotic drawer and if you need me I will be in the trauma room. Thank you for coming down hunny, and my God, you have beautiful eyes."* Then she disappeared behind the curtain in the trauma room and that concluded my first orientation to the Emergency Department.

By the time I finished all my duties including charting and reporting on all the patients I looked after, it was nearly 9:00 PM and I was only supposed to work from 7-7. The amount I learned in those fourteen hours would have taken weeks to learn on another floor simply because we rarely had the opportunity to practice so many skills in such a short period of time. And I loved every minute of it.

I was later scheduled in for more regular shifts in the ER and the Recovery Unit where I was trained to recover patients one-on-one. These patients required constant monitoring and observation until recovered enough to safely be transferred to the Surgery floor. After several months in the ER I had become very adapted to working in a fast paced and high stress environment. Soon, the nursing and critical thinking skills I had acquired here became second nature. Common scenarios such as various traumas, myocardial infarctions or "heart attacks", drug overdoses, and GI bleeds became familiar for me to see and deal with. Instead of becoming overwhelmed or panicked with anxiety in these cases I seemed to thrive and function without hesitation relying mainly on past experience and the knowledge I had obtained from the more experienced ER nurses to help guide me through. I felt that this was where I belonged and it made me feel important when I told people where I worked.

I had gotten used to the commute to and from work and enjoyed the time to myself to reflect on the events of the day as I sipped my coffee and smoked out the window. We took Macy as often as we could on my stretches off and our summer days were spent swimming at the beach, barbequing on the deck, and camping with friends who also had a little girl Macy's age. When I did not have Macy I usually organized a poker game with friends that still lived in town. The games were intense as we all played poker in university and took it pretty seriously. It was all business once we sat down and we were all there to make money. There were many mornings Lyndsay got up to go to class to find us sitting at the kitchen table at 8:00 AM still drinking and in the middle of a hand. My friend, Sheldon, would usually grin and say "Good morning Lyndsay, you have an early class today do you? That sucks!" She would just shake her head and tell him to "Frig off" then proceed to give me the look of death before she headed out the door. We would laugh our asses off for a few minutes and then get straight back to business. We always played with unlimited buy-ins, therefore as long as someone still had money in his or her pocket the game always continued. It was good times.

When Lyndsay graduated from the School of Nursing she obtained a position on GI Surgery at the Victoria General in Halifax, NS. I found a full time position on Orthopedic Surgery at the Halifax Infirmary, so with that we left the small university town of Antigonish to begin our new careers in the city of Halifax.

Halifax was only two hours from where we went to school but the lifestyle and the aura that comes with living in the city was much different, and I loved it. It reminded me of living in ON and experiencing the anonymity and freedom that one could not experience when living in a small town.

Lyndsay and I were both excited and nervous as we were on our own and both starting new jobs at big hospitals. It was only her first year as a new graduate and I only had a year experience as an RN. We did not know what the future held for us in the city. The possibilities were endless.

We settled into a beautiful apartment overlooking the Halifax harbor just outside the city located in the Royal Hemlock Ravines. We were the first tenants to live in it as it was just newly built. All the appliances were brand new and still had the cardboard sleeves inside them. I nearly ruined my scrubs when I did a load of laundry and forgot to remove the cardboard from inside the washing machine. The floors throughout the apartment were dark hardwood and it was an open concept layout that we loved right away. We splurged on our first furniture-shopping excursion and bought a beautiful leather couch and chair set. They were a rich burgundy and Lyndsay could easily lay crossways in the plush leather chair, as it was so big.

We had settled into our positions within the Capital District Health Authority, both of us becoming well respected as nurses and employees amongst our coworkers. I loved my floor and even though it was a heavy workload I thoroughly enjoyed the group of nurses I worked with. I think they liked working with me as well because they did not have to get the Hoyer lift to transfer a patient when I was working.

One of the women I worked with always wore the old fashioned nursing dress and white stockings when she came to work. All she was missing was the little hat they wore back in the old days and the "Florence Nightingale" look would have been complete. If she were to read this she would know I am just teasing her and that she was really one of my favorite nurses to work with. She was good at tormenting too and always said she hated taking over my patient load when we changed shifts because I had all the old ladies spoiled rotten. She would then begin one of her famous tirades that had everyone in hearing distance laughing hysterically. She would say something like, "I could go in that patient's room right now, bath her from head to toe, fix her hair, put her lipstick on, change her attends, and if I was wiping her behind and she farted in my face, she would not even say excuse me." By that time we were all roaring, and then she would add, "But when Ben strolls in with a cup of tea and a piece of dry toast she gets all flustered and thinks he is the best thing that has ever happened to this hospital, even though I have been here for twenty years."

I continued working there for two years and also worked many overtime shifts on the Plastics/Burn Unit. I really enjoyed my job in Halifax and given that I was only an hour and a half away from Macy worked out perfectly. The fact that both our families were living in NS also made us feel that this was our home. My dad, stepmom, and two sisters had moved again and were now only about forty-five minutes away from me. Mom still lived and worked in the town I attended university in and my brother was about to graduate from that same school that year. Lyndsay's parents also lived about an hour away from the city. It was definitely great to have them all close.

However, with our huge student loan debts, my child support payments, and our rent and other bills, it quickly became apparent that if we wanted to get ahead then a change had to be made. I was always stressed about money and it did not seem as though I was any better off than when I first graduated three years ago.

After weeks of searching for better paying jobs outside our province we both decided to apply for full-time one year contracts in a remote northern community located in the North West Territories of Canada. We both realized that the isolation accompanied with being far from our families, friends, and Macy would be very difficult and our relationship would definitely be tested like never before. A year was a huge commitment especially if we got there and hated it. But it was also an adventure and a chance to better ourselves much quicker financially than if we continued living paycheck to paycheck in NS. So we went for it.

Interviews for both Lyndsay and I went well but we were not expecting to be grilled so hard; the interview was very intense. After filling out and faxing stacks of documents we accepted the one-year contracts for positions on Acute Care in a remote community located 120 miles north of the Arctic Circle. After the initial excitement of accepting the jobs wore off we started researching where exactly it was that we were moving. No, we did not think to do this before we accepted the contracts.

We looked at pictures of the town, viewed videos that a few of the locals had posted, and then saw the weather report at the bottom of the screen. It showed the temperature to be -36 degrees Celsius, and that was without the windchill. We quickly realized then neither of us had any concept whatsoever of where it was we were actually moving.

*"As I walk the hemisphere, I got my wish to
up and disappear . . . I have been wounded,
I have been healed . . . but for landing I've
been, for landing I've been cleared."*

—Eddie Veder

The North
Chapter 10

Where in the hell are we? Our plane was about to land
and I see only frozen tundra and snow covered barrens.
Our total flight time consisted of two days travel starting
from Halifax, NS, to Toronto, ON, a brief flight change
there and then off to Edmonton, AB (Alberta). After
overnighting in Edmonton we awoke early and began
the second leg of the journey to the North.

Through the window I could tell that the early spring
weather was becoming more and more replaced by a still
ever present cold and snow covered northern winter.
From above the earth I could not help but notice how
different the landscape was in comparison to the thick and
full boreal forests of NS and NL.

It was a harsh and barren landscape and the trees were sickly and beaten, barely surviving in conditions with extreme sub-zero temperatures and very little precipitation. Vast stretches of tundra replaced the ominous mountains of the now southern Rockies. I began to wonder how living things have survived here but soon realized as I look around at the passengers of the plane, that the people, like the wildlife, are of a different breed. Northerners in general are a tough and tested group and have adapted to surviving in their environment over centuries.

I am familiar with the many indecencies they endured when many were taken from their parents and their homes and forced to attend residential schools and speak English. It sickens me to think of the abuse these people suffered at the hands of strangers and that most were not allowed to visit or even write to their families until they completed school. I think about how hard it would be to ever trust anyone again and that it would be almost impossible to break free of depression and self-loathing after what they had been through. But yet most exude a positive exterior and the ease and readiness to laugh and smile. This should not be mistaken for weakness or softness however, as beneath that exterior is a powerful readiness to fight and never flee from any threats to themselves or their families.

After a short stop in Yellowknife, NWT, we continued further north, where I saw numerous veins of frozen water that snaked across the landscape as far as the eye could see. They all seemed to branch from one massive river body, which I later found out was the great Mackenzie River and considered to be the life blood of the Beaufort-Delta region. The pilots voice came over the speaker signaling that we were about to begin the decent into the remote community of Inuvik, NWT, which we would call home for the next twelve months.

The temperature outside that day was a balmy -18 degrees Celsius and after grabbing our luggage we hopped in one of the cabs that was parked outside the airport. I found it strange that there were so many cabs in such a small town and most of the cab drivers were Middle Eastern. I wondered how in the hell they even heard about Inuvik, let alone work here.

The cab diver knew we were foreigners and offered to give us a tour of the town at no charge. He then proceeded to head straight toward the frozen river on the outside of town. I noticed a stop sign sticking out of the ice, and realized that this river was in fact an ice-road. Lyndsay and I were both freaked out at the idea of driving over a frozen river but he just laughed and assured us it was perfectly safe.

I was thankful that the volume of the radio was turned up because I did not want to hear any creaking and cracking noises like you hear on the show Ice Road Truckers. Once we had turned off the river and were safely on solid ground, Lyndsay finally opened her eyes and began to breathe again. It was definitely surreal being here and seeing with our own eyes the town that only two days ago we had been looking at pictures of on the Internet. I knew this would be the ultimate test to myself and questioned whether or not I was able to deal with the isolation and the pressure and stress of starting a new job far from home.

Can I provide this hospital and this new population, which I now serve, with positive contributions? Am I needed here and will my skills be beneficial to my employers, or do I lack what it takes to practice in this new health care setting? These are the questions I started to ask myself and, again, I feel something from deep inside me trying to reach me, to tell me what I have ignored for many years. It screams at me; "You are not well, nor are you happy with your life". "Please tell someone, talk to someone, for if you continue to ignore me I promise I will wake you with a reality that you can no longer ignore." But I feel sick to my stomach when I think of telling those closest to me how unhappy I really am. I would stand to lose all the things I believed were important to me, such as starting this new job, being able to buy my own home, paying off my student loans, as well as the pride and acknowledgment I was awarded for being successful in my career as a nurse. I successfully manage to quite this voice in my head to a faint whisper and instead focus on all the positive opportunities that surely would arise from this new career change.

We slowly settled into our new life in the North. We found a modest, single bedroom apartment in one of the cheapest buildings in town that still cost us eleven hundred dollars a month to rent. The entire apartment was about the size of the living room in our house back in Halifax leaving us with little personal space. If we happened to be fighting it meant it was going to be a long day as there were not many other places to go unless one of us was working.

The isolation combined with the stress of our new jobs and being away from family and friends caused many confrontations between Lyndsay and I. Surprisingly, we both managed to come out unscathed, which, unfortunately, cannot be said for some of the walls and the bathroom door. Luckily though, with a little plaster and paint I managed to get our damage deposit back when we left.

Eventually we stopped looking at the prices of groceries when we went shopping because I would become too depressed knowing I was paying twelve dollars for milk and almost twenty dollars per kilogram for a bag of wilted grapes. The worst was when the road closed in the spring and all groceries had to be flown in. This would cause the prices of food to skyrocket, which did not matter because we had to eat.

Both of us enjoyed working on Acute Care, which covered thirteen or so beds, two labour and delivery rooms, and a day surgery room with four stretchers reserved for patients coming and going from the operating room. Our patients ranged from obstetrical, pediatric, geriatric, surgical, medical, cardiac, psychiatric, and palliative. You name it; we treated it. This wide range of health care needs meant we had to broaden our scope of practice, and therefore, we gained experience and knowledge that is unavailable in the more specified units found in larger hospitals. Lyndsay was encouraged to take the NRP course (neonatal resuscitation) so she could receive newborns and score them based on the Apgar scale, which is based on vitals, skin color, presence of meconium, and so on. Also, the course taught how to intervene if a newborn came out "flat", meaning they needed to be suctioned and provided with oxygen immediately to help them breathe.

My role at the hospital took a different turn when, after months of working in Acute Care, I was asked if I wanted to orientate to the ER. I had experience working in emergency but I was never the sole nurse in charge.

Days were staffed with one RN and one LPN (Licensed Practical Nurse) along with the physician who was on call. Nights meant just the doctor and I were responsible for the entire department from 7:30 PM—7:30 AM. One could never predict how the shift was going to play out and, good or bad, I was responsible and had to be prepared for whatever came through the doors over those twelve hours.

I wish I could say that I conducted myself in a professional manner both in and out of the hospital and that I had become a mature, responsible, ethical, and productive member of the community. But that will never be me. I remember one night in particular a few of us guys got together and played a few games of poker, had a few drinks, and then decided to go to The Trapper, which was the only bar in town. The other guys were wary about going and understandably so as it was a bit rough but I was very convincing and finally they agreed to go. As the night went on I began shooting tequila and was at one point dancing in the middle of the dance floor by myself and having a great time. I met a few locals who liked to party and I ended up getting pretty baked as well. One of my colleagues turned a funny shade of green when we were outside the bar so I put him in a cab, gave the driver five bucks, and sent him home to his wife. That was the last time he ever went to The Trapper with us.

At that point, me and two other colleagues were just getting started and agreed to go to a house party after the bar closed at 2:00 AM. Now, these guys are not lightweights when it comes to drinking but I grew up in the Maritime's and there was no way I was going to let them out drink me. We took turns passing around several bottles of vodka each time greedily chugging it like it was water. I then started challenging the biggest guys to arm wrestling matches while the vodka and the joints kept on coming. The friend I was with had stopped drinking several hours earlier as he saw where this was going and had the foresight to stay somewhat sober. The last thing I remember was holding onto him while I puked over the side railing of a different house we ended up visiting.

I woke up the next morning and I felt extremely rough. I noticed four different holes in my arm and tried to remember how I got home from the party. Flashes of arm wrestling, vodka bottles, and public displays of affection with complete strangers, who at the time I considered to be my best friends, started to come back to me.

"You have no idea what you put us through last night, do you?" Lyndsay asked. Apparently, my friend had dragged me home and up several flights of stairs of the apartment building to my apartment. My eyes had turned black, which is the usual reaction with me when I am dangerously drunk. I had been slipping in and out of consciousness and Lyndsay had almost called the ambulance to come get me. The problem was I was about to orientate to ER a few days later so it probably would not have left a good impression on the night staff. Instead, my friend went to ER and asked for some supplies and brought them back to the apartment. He proceeded to try and get a line started on me and transfuse me with some fluids, however it would seem I am not the most cooperative of all patients. It took him several attempts to finally get one; hence the multiple holes in my arm. Lyndsay was not impressed to say the least and to the friend that got me home alive that night, thank you.

While in the North, Lyndsay and I became quite close with another couple from Halifax and as time went on we began to rely on one another for support and company. I Knew Kat from working with her previously in Halifax and I immediately liked her partner Louie, as we shared many of the same interests. He really changed my life and I have to say I am a better man these days because of him. He introduced me to the gym and would force me through a grueling workout regime as I tried to keep up with him. I remember the first full body workout he put me through; I really thought I was going to have an aneurism. After it ended I proceeded to head to the bathroom where I started vomiting from sheer exhaustion.

We both also had a real passion for cooking and there was an unspoken rivalry for who could outdo the other in the kitchen. I think I have to give the edge to him but only because of his plate presentation. However, if you want to feel full after you eat, I am your man. Roasted beet salads and pureed soups just did not cut it, sorry Louis.

And then there were the heated poker games we would organize and that is where our friendship would briefly be put on hold. He was my nemesis and we would always find ourselves in massive pots together, even though we promised to stay away from each other prior to the game. But the more top shelf rum we ingested, the more the competition between us grew.

There was one other player who loved the game even more than us. What made him dangerous was his utter disregard for money and what appeared to be a severe gambling addiction. He was a member of the local police force but when he was at a table with poker chips in front of him he mutated into Johnny Chan. Louie and I would lick our chops when we knew he was playing as this meant the amount of money we could make increased by a hundred-fold.

One night in particular he had an unusually bad run of cards and started using pieces of paper as I.O.U's for actual cash. In the end, he ran out of paper, and I had left with a week of his pay and a pocket full of crumpled pieces of paper that totalled another thousand dollars. We really crushed him that night, both spiritually and financially. We did not see him for a few weeks after that experience.

I am confident it was a little embarrassing for a police officer to have to come into the ER and pay a nurse the thousand dollars he still owed him from poker. But he was a class act and even counted out the money for me on top of the nursing station front desk. I am sure the student who I was orientating thought I was in the mafia as she watched a uniformed officer of the law hand over almost a weeks pay to me.

And I cannot forget to mention the bingo games that were broadcast on the local community station. I think it was Louie who first discovered them and, let me tell you, the locals loved their bingo. The line-ups for the cards were ridiculous and the cash prizes were huge especially the one on Saturday, which was never less than ten thousand dollars. I never understood how the prizes could be so big when the community was so small but to understand that you have to see the people there play bingo. Even the patients at the hospital who were very sick or just had an operation would shuffle out to the TV room with their bingo cards and dabbers in hand. Some people had four to six cards and each card had six individual games on it.

I attempted this once when Louie was late coming over and the lady started calling out the numbers. I had to cover my three sheets and Louie's three at the same time. By the time he had arrived I had consumed about eight Coronas, smoked a half pack of cigarettes, spilt one of the beers over the cards, and called the station about five times to politely ask the announcer to slow down. This caused her to speed up reading out the numbers and I was beginning to sweat because I had been standing the entire time dabbing out numbers like a madman. I felt like an air control operator at the Los Angeles International airport. When Louie strolled in and asked, "Oh, it started already?" I barely resisted the urge to throw the dabber at my inquisitive looking friend. Neither of us ever won anything during all those years playing bingo so I think I will just stick to poker.

"I hurt myself today, to see if I still feel. I focus on the pain, the only thing that's real. The needle tears a hole, the old familiar sting. Try to kill it all away, but I remember everything".

-Johnny Cash.

Secrets
Chapter 11

I remember clearly the first time I decided to inject myself with narcotics. Our year contract was over but we extended it for another two months and I had been working in the ER for several months by then. After a three-week vacation back in Halifax we signed on for several more contracts that were for three to four months at a time with a few weeks off in between to go back home.

I had been taking care of a patient that was known as a "frequent flyer" at the emergency department. It was a night shift and she was my only patient at the time, which allowed me to spoil her with warm blankets, cups of tea, and lots of time to sit and talk. She had an order for 5-7.5 mg of morphine to be given intramuscularly every fifteen minutes for pain PRN (as needed). This was a high frequency for such a large dose but she had built up quite a tolerance for the drug and seemed to sincerely be in discomfort when she came to the ER.

I had given her the usual 5 mg of morphine in her hip and rather than wasting the remaining 5 mg or saving it for when she needed it again, I convinced myself I was going to take it. I think my decision was partly out of curiosity, wondering what it felt like, and watching how it made others feel better. But I also knew I had not been happy with many things in my life and was slowly becoming more and more depressed without even realizing it.

I snuck into one of the empty rooms, attached a sterile 30-gauge needle to the syringe, and slowly pushed the liquid into my abdominal fold. Being a nurse, I knew that by doing it subcutaneously it would be more slowly absorbed into my blood system thereby not affecting me as much as an intravenous dose would. I immediately regretted doing this as I soon became paranoid with the thoughts of having a reaction or becoming sedated by it. After all, I still had to give report to the morning nurse coming on shift. This was the first experience I ever had with opioids. High school and university had provided me with lots of experience smoking weed and hash but never anything hard like cocaine or methamphetamine.

When I was in grade nine and young and stupid, I did try acid. The feeling of losing control honestly scared the shit out of me, enough so, that I had never tried it since. So, why now, at the age of 29 and four years into my nursing career, had I just injected myself with morphine? I know this substance is highly powerful and highly addictive. I also know all my instincts are telling me it is wrong and if I were caught I would surely lose my job.

"What are you doing? This isn't you. Talk to someone. Tell them you are unhappy. Tell them you're not well." The voice is there again, and once again I ignored it.

The morphine felt like a bee sting when it entered my tissue but after a few minutes it gradually faded. The pain was replaced by a warm sensation that spread through my body and settled into my head. My eyes felt heavier and looked almost glasslike in the mirror. A calming peacefulness began to sweep over me. I took a deep breath in and slowly breathed out. The feeling I got was great. My first thought after I managed to ignore the guilt and initial paranoia was, "I'm not allergic". My next thought was that I still had control; at least I thought I did, over my thoughts and actions. I had not yet thought about how it would affect my ability to function as a nurse. What if a major trauma arrives that requires specific and immediate interventions? I have to be able to think clear and critical thinking and multitasking are a huge part of my job, especially in the ER.

As time went on my drug use escalated, along with my tolerance. Because of my access to and familiarity with drugs, I grew comfortable using them on my own. I saw for myself that drugs help people feel better and can solve problems. I began to think that, because of my knowledge and experience as a nurse, I could self-medicate without becoming addicted. I really believed that I did not have a drug problem and that I could stop if I wanted to; that it was still my choice. Even today I believe I had a choice but that choice became harder and harder to make as my drug use continued. I just did not realize it then. After all, I was a nurse; I knew what I was doing. I assured myself that if it affected my job or my life outside work then I would stop. Even after using for two years and my addiction worsening, I believed I could stop if I wanted to. It was not until I was caught that I realized there was no possibility of ever stopping on my own. If I did not hit that proverbial wall or get caught I would still be using every day and still working in the ER.

I was telling myself that because I was not using intravenously, I was not an addict. I cannot explain how the euphoria that I felt from the drugs had by this time changed to a feeling of being normal. It was as familiar to me as smoking or drinking coffee, just another part of everyday life. And I knew I could never, ever, tell a soul. So I did not.

I continued with my life outside the hospital as usual but gradually the drug use became more and more a part of that world too. I still continued going to the gym with Louie, usually going to the bathroom to inject myself. I kept a syringe prefilled with demerol, morphine, or dilaudid hidden in my knapsack. After injecting myself I would return to lifting weights and finishing my workout.

The poker games continued also and I always made sure to bring enough injectable narcotics to last through a game. I had become used to drinking heavily while using as well and no one ever noticed a change in my behaviour, at least not that I knew. A few of these games were even held at the home of a member of the local police force or at their mess hall.

When I was at home was the worse, especially when Lyndsay went to work and I was alone. I made sure to stock pile enough to last the weekend, rationing it by taking only half a vial every 1-2 hours, give or take. The dose in milligrams depended on the drug. Demerol was

100 mg/ml, morphine was 10 mg/ml, and the dilaudid (hydromorphine) vials were 2 mg/ml, as it was almost 6-8 times the strength of morphine.

I had become more and more daring with the unlawful means I used to get the drugs as well. I had progressed from taking wastages to making up patients who were not even there and signing their names to the pharmacy sheets. However, my main means of obtaining it was by destroying the entire sheet and making up a new count after taking what I needed. Nothing fazed me anymore and I simply got used to this, almost thinking I deserved it.

I began to condone my drug use because everyone kept praising me for being a great nurse. I told myself I was not really addicted because after each contract I would return to Halifax and simply stop, just like that. I would fill my time visiting with my daughter, Mom, Dad and Kara, and our friends, all of which work in the health care field. I knew I craved it and if I had it I would have used, but I did not have access to it in Halifax so I simply went without. I was truly leading a double life and the weight of this secret was beginning to become unbearable.

During Christmas, 2010, an event so traumatic occurred, that our lives would change forever. We were housesitting for a friend and while I was getting ready to go to work, Lyndsay was on the computer checking her Facebook account. I heard her scream, "Oh my God!" and ran into the spare bedroom to see what was going on. A relative of hers had posted on her wall, "I am so sorry to hear about Joe", but Lyndsay had no idea what he was talking about. Joe or "Puppy Joe", as Lyndsay affectionately called him was her grandfather, a sweet gentleman who lived on his own in an apartment in Sackville, NS. We immediately thought the worse and assumed he had passed as his COPD had become more and more problematic the past few years. I told her not to panic and to try and reach someone from her family. I had to go to work and relieve the night nurse but told her to call me as soon as she heard something.

It was about fifteen minutes after I arrived at work that she called me, hysterical. I cannot recall how she discovered the article in the Halifax newspaper online but nothing could have prepared her for what she read. The article showed a picture of the building that she immediately recognized as the one her grandfather lived in. It described how the police were investigating a grisly murder of an elderly man in an apartment building in Lower Sackville, NS.

Her and our close friend Melissa came over to the ER and I got one of the doctors to order her several ativan, as well as a few to take with her. As I signed out the ativan, I also made up a new narcotic control sheet and took all the demerol and morphine that I could without it being too noticeable. Then I put the old sheet into my pocket and told a co-worker that I needed to get the hell out of there and take Lyndsay back home.

She showed me the article on the CBC website which read, and I quote *"A charge has been laid in Fridays grisly murder of a 73-year-old man in Lower Sackville, N.S. Nicolas Edward White, 24, is in custody on a second-degree murder charge. The accused and the victim lived in the same apartment building at 70 Cobequid Road. 'It's no secret for anybody that lives down there, there was quite a blood trail involved,' said Staff Sgt. Peter Ferguson. He added that police are still processing the scene. Police believe that not long after the homicide, White was trying to break into an apartment in a nearby building. A bloody trail led officers to a cemetery where the accused was chased down and a weapon found."*

We were in shock to say the least, and Lyndsay frantically began calling other family to see if anyone knew anything more. She did not understand why no one contacted her, as the murder took place several days prior. She also could not be certain that it was "Puppy Joe", since no name was yet released.

But it had been him, and we later found out all the facts surrounding the murder from a detective who was on the case. They needed a next of kin to identify Joe, but Lyndsay informed them that all his family were living either in the west or up north, besides his sisters in Halifax. The detective also described how Joe had been brutally stabbed numerous times and therefore did not want any family to have to see him if it could be avoided.

We spent the next few days at home and Melissa decided to stay as well; she was a wonderful support to Lyndsay. She had also been through a very similar experience with the murder of her uncle, and knew exactly what kind of pain Lyndsay was feeling.

I cooked for us all the rest of the week and drank heavily over the course of that week too but discovered I could not get drunk no matter how much alcohol I consumed. The news was so surreal that I felt like I was in a dream state for days. But I had a handful of vials in my parka jacket and they helped me stay good and numb throughout the week until I had to go back to work.

Lyndsay flew home to Halifax to be with the rest of her family who were making the trip back for the funeral as well. I stayed in Inuvik, but took another week off and got high every day. It helped me forget about the fact that we were supposed to have him over for Christmas dinner when we went home. I still have trouble talking about it because I know all the grisly details, as we attended several of the court proceeding surrounding the murder.

Obviously, I cannot discuss the case because undoubtedly the lawyer defending him would use it as a way to get him off. So I can only state the facts as well as express my personal opinion of the guy who is charged with murdering my wife's elderly grandfather. So, to the piece of shit coward who liked to stare and smirk at us when we were in court, I hope you get gangbanged and donkey punched in the back of the head every night if they release you into the general population. If you did kill him, then I want to know why? At least have the decency and courage to tell those who are mourning the loss of such a gentle human being such as Joe. He was a kind man, who walked with a cane and wore a cowboy hat, and was liked by so many people because even though he did not have much, he was generous with what he did have. However, if you did not murder this innocent man, then I apologize for the nasty remarks; I just get very emotional when I revisit this experience in my head.

As of today the trial continues. The suspect pled not guilty to the murder, and it remains one of the most gut-wrenching experiences of our lives.

As hard as it is to write this book, knowing it will hurt some of those closest to me, it can never be as difficult as that day when we found out Joe was murdered. That is why I have the strength and drive to keep writing, because life is too short to continue holding things in.

My brother Jeff and I in 1984, Harrington Harbour, Quebec.

Me at age four, Harrington Harbour, Quebec.

Dad, Lower North Shore, Quebec.

Mom. Lower North Shore, Quebec.

Mama and Papa, Harrington Harbour, Quebec.

L-R. Papa, Dad, and Uncle Randy,
aboard the Cape Airey. Harrington Harbour, Quebec.

L-R. My brother Jeff C., Jeremy C., Mandy R., Lucinda C., Lynn R., Jessica C., and me. Harrington Harbour, Quebec.

Dwayne and I anxiously waiting for Jeff to blow out his candles. St. Anthony, NL.

Chatting to Dwayne outside my house. St. Anthony, NL.

Dwayne getting ready to spar in a karate tournament.
Corner Brook, NL.

The house I grew up in. St. Anthony, NL.

Me in 1988. St. Anthony, NL.

"Little" Ben H., James H., Jeff C., and me
on summer vacation. Gros Morne National Park, NL.

My brother Jeff and me. St. Anthony, NL.

My brother Jeff and me on the hill behind our house.
St. Anthony, NL.

My parents and us a year before they separated.
St. Anthony, NL.

Dad and I. St. Anthony, NL.

Me in our new apartment after my parents' separation.
St. Anthony, NL.

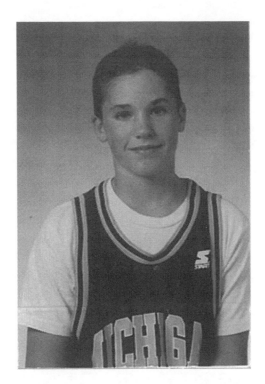

Me in Ontario about a year after leaving St. Anthony.

Jeff, Grandma, and me at Mom's graduation
from McMaster University. Hamilton, Ont.

Me after moving for the second time to Ingonish,
Cape Breton.

Me shortly before I went to live with Dad in Roddickton, NL.

Me a year after moving to Roddickton, NL.

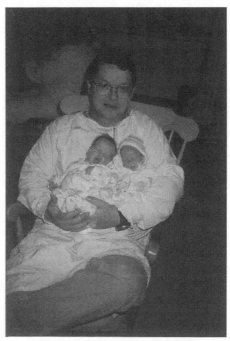

Dad and my twin sisters at the hospital in St. John's, NL.

Me in 1988 at Signal Hill, St. John's, NL.

Me in 1999, right after high school graduation.

Me and my roomates at X-Ring Ceremony,
Saint Francis Xavier University, NS.

Mom and I on graduation day
from Saint Francis Xavier University, NS.

Ben . . . RN!! Inuvik, NWT, 2009.

Where I worked for almost four years.
Inuvik Regional Hospital, NWT.

Me on the Mackenzie River, Inuvik, NWT.

Bingo and beers, a normal day off. Inuvik, NWT.

My grandfather "Papa" and me. Chester, NS.

Me at my house in Halifax a few months
before flying to Inuvik for sentencing.

*"You and tequila make me crazy; run like poison
in my blood. One more night could kill me baby,
one is one too many, one more is never enough."*

—*Kenny Chesney*

Mexico
Chapter 12

Several months had passed since Lyndsay's grandfather
was murdered and we needed a vacation to take our minds
off the court hearings surrounding the murder. My in-
laws decided to take and one of Lyndsay's closest friends
to Mexico for a relaxing stay at an all-expense paid resort
in Cancun, Mexico.

The first few days there were wonderful. It was heaven
with beautiful beaches, the clear blue ocean, and my
favourite part; of course, the all you can drink poolside
bars. They probably should have had restrictions for
anyone from the Maritime's because I definitely put a
large dent in their rum and tequila stocks.

Despite all the luxuries on the resort, I was still not
well and found myself to be particularly irritable with
those around me. Maybe it was because I did not have

a buddy to hang out with or maybe because I had gone several weeks without injecting myself, but whatever the reason, I just could not seem to enjoy myself.

I ventured off several times in search of some adventure and I found it in the form of a local who was hanging out by the boardwalk. He approached me and asked if I needed some marijuana and I replied "Sure!" Then he asked if I wanted something else and proceeded to show me a bag full of little vials filled with cocaine. He was charging eighty American dollars for each vial but said he would give me five for three hundred American dollars. Even though I did not snort cocaine and only tried it once at a bachelor party, without hesitation I told him I would take the five. So, with my quarter ounce of weed and five grams of cocaine I made my way back to the hotel room, stashed most of it, rolled a joint, and snorted two generous lines of the cocaine.

At this point in my life I had spent almost two years building a tolerance to strong narcotics and as long as it was not rat poison I figured I could easily handle the cocaine. And I was right; it felt amazing. Not as good as the prescription drugs, but pretty damn close. I looked in the mirror at my eyes were more piercing blue than ever and I felt like I could do anything. I strolled out of the room wearing just my shorts and sandals and made my way towards one of the pool bars.

At the bar I ordered two large glasses of rum and coke and chugged two tequila shots while I waited. I felt like Tony Montana must have felt when he was on top of the world in the movie Scarface and my confidence was at an all-time high. I felt invincible and my body was tense and shook with adrenaline. I ignored the people I travelled with and instead hung out by the pool and bar meeting new people and making friends with complete strangers from all over the world. I felt alive for the first time on this trip; I felt free.

The day continued on like this and no amount of alcohol was getting me tipsy. I pounded back tequila shots with tabasco sauce like they were water. My father-in-law joined me by the bar and tried to catch up to the abuse I was inflicting on my liver. Eventually, I ended up in the pool acting like a maniac and scared off many of the sober guests. By the time my wife and the rest of our group showed up I had already made friends with a bunch of Russians, Spaniards, and all the bartenders. Even though I could not understand a thing they were saying we had our arms around each other singing to the music and taking turns ordering rounds of drinks. What ensued next are events that I have no recollection of and I am only going by what others told me.

Apparently, both my father-in-law and I were now hugging each other and could barely open our eyes. I thought I lost my university 'X' ring in the pool and almost drowned while looking for it. I started to cry and curse when I thought it was gone, even though my mother-in-law tried to tell me I had given it to her. I then proceeded to walk back to the bar and help myself to the bottle of tequila that was behind the counter. The bartender just laughed at me as I greedily drank from the bottle and then shook the tabasco into my mouth to mix with the tequila before swallowing.

At that point everyone thought it would be a good idea to try and escort my father-in-law and I back to our rooms but let me tell you, this turned out to be anything but a simple task. I delivered a haymaker right hand to the elevator door because it was not taking us up fast enough. Once I got to the room I karate kicked the door and put my foot straight through it just as Lyndsay was about to insert the key. Once inside I started sobbing and cried, "You guys don't know me, no one knows me. I am not a good person; you don't know what I have done. Nobody does, FUUUUUUUUCK!" I kicked the bed so hard I sent it slamming into the wall and then picked up the old model box television set and threw it across the room. I had lost all control and my eyes turned from blue to black. My in-laws came down from upstairs to try and get me settled but by that time I was already passed out on the bed.

My father-in-law was pretty intoxicated as well and tried to defend me by giving both Lyndsay and her friend crap for not letting me continue drinking at the pool bar. It was not until he mentioned the words "Stop acting like a snobby little bitch", that I snapped out of my semi-comatose state. I sprang out of bed and lunged for my father-in-law and threw him across the room, ripping his shirt completely off him in the process. I stood over him with all three women crying and holding me by the arms while I screamed, "If you ever talk like that to her again, I will not be able to control what I do, OK? I will kick you in the fucking teeth if you say one more word to my wife, do you hear me? Now please, for your sake, get out of our room." Both my in-laws exited through the door with the hole in it and I resumed passing out on one of the double beds. There I sobbed for almost an hour until finally drifting off into a deep sleep.

When I awoke the next morning it took me about twenty minutes to fully open my eyes. It took another twenty minutes to force myself to get out of bed and head straight for the shower. On the way to the bathroom I stepped over the large television that was lying face down in the center of the room, once there, I turned on the shower, stepped in, and sat down on the cold tile floor. As I was sitting there, flashes of the chaos that arose the night prior were running through my head and I could not be sure what was real and what was imagined. It was not until I reached for the shampoo that I noticed my arm. It was swollen to twice its normal size with a large hematoma developing over the posterior area of my wrist. I tried to make a fist but the pain that immediately shot through my arm deterred me from any further attempts. What or who did I hit last night?

After finding out from Lyndsay what transpired and how my injury was the result of a one-sided battle with an elevator door, we packed our suitcases and headed down the lobby to meet up with her parents. Seeing them was probably the most awkward moment of my life, as none of us really knew what to say. My mother-in-law was the first to speak, cheerfully saying, "Gee, it sure is a beautiful morning, sure wish we could stay for another week. That was a lot of fun!" The rest of us just stared at her blankly, and I wondered to myself, "What the hell is she talking about?"

Lyndsay went to the front desk to check out and that is when they laid out three photos taken of me kicking the door to the room. There was a camera in every hallway, which tells me I am probably not the first guy to lose his shit in Mexico.

The only thing Lyndsay could do was to ask how much we owed for the damages to the room. There was obviously no disputing what I had done considering she had laid out in front of her three pictures of me in action. The total bill for damages was a thousand dollars to which she charged on her MasterCard. They then advised her that it was probably in my best interest to never visit this resort again.

The bus ride to the airport had not been any less awkward and it was not until we landed in Toronto, ON, and had to say our goodbyes that we finally spoke to each other. I just wanted to get back home as my wrist was starting to get tighter and had now begun to throb constantly. An x-ray later confirmed a fracture of the wrist and I was fitted with a wrist splint that had to be worn for 6 weeks.

When we finally arrived back in Halifax we discovered that my grandfather had been sent to the Valley Regional Hospital for a surgery consult regarding an ulcer on his foot. The wound had not responded well to antibiotics and the infection had continuously worsened. His doctor and the surgeon sat down with both my parents and grandmother and gave them the options that were available to them. They had a discussion about performing a below the knee amputation but decided instead on a less aggressive procedure where they would debride the infected tissue around the wound. A below the knee amputation would simply render Papa bed ridden, as this was his only good leg. Once they debrided the ulcer in surgery and he returned to the floor, Papa began to become very short of breath and extremely confused. The surgeons were questioning whether or not he developed a blood clot or pneumonia post-operatively. My parents, however, suspected it was the result of CHF (Congestive Heart Failure) due to the fluid overload from the IV fluids required in surgery. He became more and more congested and confused, despite the IV diuretics and the oxygen. He was kept as comfortable as possible with pain medication and ativan around the clock. They continued to treat his CHF symptomatically with oxygen and Lasix and ensured that he was in the least amount of distress and discomfort possible. He would be categorized as comfort measures only and that meant if his heart stopped they would not try to resuscitate him. They would simply keep Papa pain free as the life gradually left his aging heart and body.

The family alternated in shifts and spent his last few days by his side, hugging and comforting the man who had once been so strong and so full of life. I will always be grateful for being there to sit with him during his last days of life. I always had regrets for not making more of an effort to sit and talk with him, play crib, or listen to his stories. I wanted to take this opportunity to give him back some of the time and love he had given me as a boy. I did not want him to be alone for a second even if he did not know where he was at the time.

Papa continued to deteriorate very quickly over those few days and would not even take a bite of his fish and chips I brought him, which had always been his favourite meal. He would order it every time we went out and I do not know if it was because he knew it drove everyone crazy or because he loved fresh fish and homemade fries.

We could not leave him for a minute as he grew more and more restless and agitated. He hated the oxygen mask and ripped it off his face whenever he got the chance. This caused his oxygen saturation to plummet into the low 40-50% where the oxygen saturation of an average person normally ranged from 95-100%.

His face and lips were now beginning to change from pink to a more purplish color and even with the facemask set at the highest flow level, his oxygen levels remained dangerously low. The morphine and ativan seemed to calm him and settle him nicely so we had the doctor increase the frequency of his doses to ensure they lasted him longer. He still needed someone by him at all times as he would frequently try and get up on his own. Even with the oxygen and the painkillers he could not get comfortable at times and despite the fact that I am a nurse and quite used to seeing people in discomfort, I hated having to see Papa like this.

But I knew he was still in there somewhere. My grandmother and I were sitting with him one day and he kept pulling at the blankets and sheets, twisting them and trying desperately to tie them over and over. I held his hands in mine so he would not yank out his IV or catheter and I tried to explain to him why he should not pull at the sheets. Initially he would agree to stop but then go right back to yanking and pulling at them. It was not until later that we figured out he was trying to mend his fishing nets, something he spent endless hours doing in his shed. He was doing what came natural to him, what his hands knew how to do from years and years of practice and repetition.

This was a man who spent his whole life working hard to make a living from the sea and here he was in a hospital bed, confused and dying, and yet still could not stop working. That was my grandfather.

There was some talk about transferring him to Lunenburg, NS, so he could stay in one of the spacious rooms on the Palliative Care floor. But the thought of transferring him again did not sit right with my family; therefore the decision was made to turn back his oxygen. Dad and Mama stayed with him through the night while I went home to catch up on some sleep. I drove back to the hospital early the next morning to see him and bought with me some gin and tonic so I could sneak him a little sniff of his favourite drink, as well as enough plastic cups for everyone else to have one. After all, I was not sure how much longer I would have with him and I did not mind breaking a few rules if it meant putting even the slightest grin on Papa's face. I walked into his room and by the looks on everyone's faces I knew he was gone. I went over to him and kissed his cheek and sniffed his aftershave as I always did, and even though his skin was cold, he still smelled like Papa.

We spent a long time in his room telling stories and sharing the gin that I brought with me and for a short while we pretended to be standing around Papa's kitchen, sharing stories and having a drink. For a moment I think we all pretended he was still there with us, tormenting and grinning at us while we sipped our drinks.

I am thankful I got to spend those last days of his life with him but I am more thankful that he is not alive to read this book and learn my darkest secrets. I know that before he left this earth his last memories of me were only good and he was proud to call me his grandson. And I am proud to call him my grandfather. I miss you Papa.

Shortly after Papa's passing, Lyndsay and I flew back to Inuvik and I fell right back into my usual routine of working hard, saving lives, caring for others, and injecting myself every day and night with narcotics. And for the next few months that followed, those summed up the events of my life, until the day came when everything fell apart.

"You can run on for a long time, but sooner or later God will cut you down, sooner or later God'll cut you down."

-Johnny Cash

No More Secrets
Chapter 13

The morning started like any other morning that I had to go to work. The alarm went off at 6:00 AM and I hit the snooze button. This gave me the extra fifteen minutes I needed to realize I had to leave the comfort of my goose down duvet and drag myself to the shower which was my only way to fully wake up and prepare for the day. As I showered my mind began to play out the day that awaited me. I knew from past experience that I could not predict exactly what the day would be like as there were multiple factors that would determine that.

First, it depended who was on shift at the hospital the night before. That played a crucial role because, depending on the nurse, the Emergency department could either be in total chaos or it could be a blank slate for me to work with, with my only worries being what came through those doors after I arrived.

I picked out a pair of fresh scrubs and put on a fresh pot of coffee. As I waited for the coffee to brew I got into nurse mode and as I went over the possible scenarios I could encounter when I arrived to the ER, I become aware that there are not many situations that I could not handle. This was my world, where I had proven time and time again that I could be depended on to deal with whatever came through those doors. Whether it was a patient with chest pain, a severe asthma attack, a GI Bleed, a threatened abortion, a seizure, a newborn with bronchitis, a severe anaphylactic reaction, a trauma, or an attempted suicide, I was ready. I knew that these were all things I was very familiar with treating and had dealt with on numerous occasions. I thought I was ready for anything. I was wrong.

I gulped down my first cup of coffee and baileys and took my second cup out onto the patio of the house we were looking after, so I could enjoy it with a cigarette, which was always my morning routine before heading to work. As usual, the little dog we were sitting followed me like a shadow and hated it when I left its sight. After taking a few deep draws on the cigarette, I reached into the inside pocket of my jacket until my fingers felt the familiar shape of the syringe then I proceeded to complete my other morning ritual.

As usual, I barely felt the 30-gauge needle enter into the subcutaneous tissue on my abdomen, as it was the smallest gauge the hospital carried. The needle being so narrow always required a steady pressure to push the liquid through the syringe but it left hardly any trace of a puncture mark or bruising as the larger needles did. The sting of the dilaudid entering my tissue, however, was unmistakable, but I had grown to like the pain because it was a precursor to the calm peaceful glow that was always sure to follow.

Satisfied, I re-capped the needle on the empty syringe and put it back in my inside pocket so I could dispose of it in the sharps container at work, then I chugged what was left of the coffee and took one last puff of my cigarette. I looked at my watch and see its time to start making my way over to ER and relieve the night nurse coming off his or her shift. Again, I start to wonder who worked last night and what sort of scene awaited me when I arrived. I placed the empty mug in the sink, gave the dog a few treats, locked the door and made my way toward the hospital located just a few minutes walking distance from the house.

I entered through the front doors and briefly spoke to the gentleman answering the telephones at the front desk. As I walked through the Acute Care ward I heard Lyndsay's voice coming from one of the patient's rooms but she sounded busy so I kept walking down the hallway and into the ER. I arrived to find the department very quiet and by looking at all the empty slots above the desk to show which patients are in what rooms, I could tell the place was empty.

"You're here early", said the night nurse who I had hoped was working. Everything was tidy and in its place, a clean slate for me to work with. God love her. I threw my coat in the med room and sat down waiting to get a report from her. Once she left the department I did my usual check of all the rooms and made sure all the equipment was functioning properly such as the oxygen flow meters, wall suctioning, and the two separate crash carts we had in the ER. I also emptied all the garbage cans from each room because I hated the sight of overflowing garbage containers and simply refused to wait for housekeeping, as they were often short-staffed and very busy. I knew most of the staff really well and I think they appreciated the gesture, which I could only do when it was quiet in the department. Also, it gave Billy and I more opportunities to share a coffee and a smoke when he came in during the morning, a tradition that we had been doing for several years, as I was one of the only ER nurses that smoked cigarettes. I had known him the longest out of all the housekeeping staff and from our many chats while outside for a smoke break I knew he was a good husband, loved his kids, rarely missed work, and was one of the most reliable and hardest workers employed at the hospital.

On that particular day though, my friend was off, and I had started to think about my next injection, as the effects of the morning dose were slowly fading. I headed into the med room and scanned the narcotic sheets to see what my options were for obtaining more of what I had come to depend on. Over the past years I had come to rely on several different means to get what I needed. In this case I saw the name of a patient who received morphine that night but was discharged from the ER several hours before I came on. I decided to sign out another vial for him even though it was not meant for him at all.

I made sure no one was around and proceeded to attach a large bore needle to a 3 cc (or 3 milliliter) syringe. Then I cracked the vial, drew up the clear liquid, discarded the vial in the sharps container, removed the large bore needle and replaced it with one used for subcutaneous injections. I grabbed an alcohol swab, went into the bathroom located in the ICU, swabbed a site on my belly, and injected half of the 100 mg vial into my skin.

For me, this was a routine that had become as familiar as brushing my teeth and the paranoia and anxiety that I had experienced when I first started using narcotics was long gone. I hid the remainder of the drug in a drawer that was seldom used and headed back out to the front desk where I see the acting nurse manager, Sue, waiting for me. "Do you have anyone here now?" she asks. I told her I did not and that I was just using the bathroom.

She asked me where the other nurse, Trish, was and I told her she should be arriving soon. I asked her if she would mind if I went out for a smoke and she said she did not mind. As I was outside smoking I could start to feel the full effect of the morphine and my entire body became very relaxed as the warm sensation spread up my neck and into my head. I felt amazing. I finished off the cigarette and headed back in to find that Trish was now occupying the chair Sue had been sitting in when I left.

Trish greeted me with a warm smile and said "Hello darling, I think we should have a good day today with the two of us on". She was one of my favourite nurses to work with and we had developed a strong trust in each other's capabilities as ER nurses during the past few years.

The phone started ringing and I answered it to hear Sue's voice telling me she needed to see me in the office. I thought nothing of it and told Trish that I would be back in a minute.

When I arrived at the office I found Sue along with the Director of Patient Care sitting at the desk and immediately I had a sick feeling because of the serious expressions on both their faces. The day had finally come.

The Director began to inform me that they had to put me on immediate suspension and proceeded to read from a formal letter that explained in detail the grounds for the suspension. The letter stated that I was to be placed on immediate suspension pending an investigation into missing narcotic control sheets, 43 to be exact, which extended over a two-year period. It was deemed I looked most suspicious as my signature was at the start of most of the new sheets, indicating I had been the nurse who transferred the count over from the sheets that were missing to the new ones.

I can recall the feeling I had as this was being read to me by the disappointed and genuinely anguished voices of my superiors. It was a feeling of leaving my body and watching myself sit there silently, nodding here and there after their sentences, but not really listening to them. I also remember hearing another voice in my head while this was happening. That voice was mine, a voice that I had managed to quiet for many years. This voice is screaming at me, *"What have you done, Jesus Christ, what the fuck have you done? You should have listened to me, remember, when I told you that you are not well, you are not happy with your life. If you had only listened to me, to yourself, and just told someone what you were feeling inside, you would not be sitting here in this office. You have to tell them everything. No more secrets. This is your chance to stop pretending that everything is okay. It is time you tell people the truth."* I tried to let the reality of what was happening sink in and it felt like minutes passed by before anyone spoke.

"Is there anything you would like to tell us, Ben?" the Director asked. I tried to speak but my mouth was dry and I could not catch my breath. Deep down I knew this day would come, when the dark secrets of my life would come out for others to see. It was inevitable. But it had been so long that I had kept my addiction to myself that it had transformed into a part of me now, a living thing that would not be ignored.

The Director saw the shock in my face and said to me, *"Why don't you go home and collect your thoughts and if you feel like talking later just call. We want to help you anyway we can. Right now this stays between us and nobody else knows that you are suspended, other than you, me, Sue (the supervisor), and Mark (the pharmacist). I want you to know that this is by far the hardest thing I have ever had to do."*

My head was spinning and I agreed to go home for a while. I was escorted back to the ER where they had already asked Trish to cover for me. Trish looked at me and asked if I was okay. My eyes started to fill up and I looked away telling her I was, in fact, not okay. I collected my clothes, which were in the med room and I knew Sue was watching me closely. I knew I had to get out of there, I had to tell my wife that I had been suspended and then I have to tell her as well as my family and my closest friends that I have been stealing and using narcotics at work for over two years. Oh God, what have I done?

Before leaving the hospital I remembered what I had stashed in the drawer before getting called down to the office. I asked Sue if I could use the bathroom but instead I snuck into the ICU, which was empty, and pull the syringe out from the drawer. I had almost forgotten about it but then I realized that this was perhaps the last time I would ever get to feel that familiar sting and the warm sensation of the liquid as it worked its way into my body. I took the syringe and proceeded to the bathroom where

I lifted my scrub top and injected the last of the morphine into my abdomen. Once again, the familiar warmth had reached my neck, my eyes felt glassed over, and I felt calm. I felt at peace. The harsh reality of what had just happened melted away, if only for a few brief minutes. I was thankful I saved one last syringe.

What was wrong with me? I had just been suspended and somehow thought that this drug is going to help me deal better with what I have to face. It was at this point in my life that I truly realized I was powerless over my addiction. I needed help.

I walked out of the ER and past the security guard at the front who asked me where I was going, but I did not provide an answer. I exited out the front doors and into the cool morning air outside. I walked past several homeless people who I recognized and one asked me for a cigarette, which I provided him. I lit his, then mine, and kept walking across the hospital parking lot and toward the house we were looking after for our nurse manager, who was away on vacation.

By then Lyndsay was fast asleep after just finishing her second 12-hour night shift and she still had two more go. I thought to myself that she would not be going into work tonight, however; not after I tell her that I have just ruined everything we had worked so hard for. Not after I tell her I have been using drugs to forget how unhappy I was, with our marriage, and with my life. I knew I had to tell her. No more hiding. Now the hard work begins.

I was still feeling the effects of the last injection but a familiar anxiety had started to replace the peaceful numbness of the morphine. I told myself, "Remember who you were, the good in you. The lives you have saved. Remember you are a good father, and you have loving and supportive parents who will help you through this. Be honest. Stay strong. Breathe. You are ready."

Cops are here!
Chapter 14

To understand how my wife truly felt, try to put yourself in her place for a moment. Imagine you have been with a man you love for over eight years. You helped raise his little girl since she was born and she called you Mommy Lyndsay since she could first talk. You worked together in the north for almost four years. He bought you a ring and got on his knees in front of his family, told you he loved you, and that he wanted to marry you. You had an amazing wedding with all your family and friends, and it was everything you ever dreamed of. You also bought a beautiful new house with him and wanted to make it your home. You knew this person well, inside and out. You knew what he liked and how to please him. And he knew how to please you. You loved him and you were happy with him.

Then one morning after you have just finished a night shift at work he came home and woke you up while you were sleeping. You wonder why he is home so early and why there were tears in his eyes. He tells you he is sorry.

He tells you he lost his job and really fucked up. He tells you he has been addicted to narcotics for two years and has been feeding his addiction by stealing drugs from the hospital. He tells you he has forged many signatures, including yours to get what he needs. He tells you he will be charged and probably go to jail. You were in shock and thought you were dreaming, and you asked him "Why?" He tells you he has been unhappy with his life, marriage, and his career for a long time. He tells you he was not sure he married you for the right reasons. He tells you he did it for you, to please you because he thought you deserved it. He tells you he cares so much for you it hurts, but he is not in love with you.

The man you thought you knew and whom you loved so much has just told you all this. You are far away from your family and friends you rely on for support and you still have to live with him and go to work for the next month until your contract is over. You think you are going to throw up when he holds you and says he is so sorry. You think maybe something is wrong with you, and feel very inadequate. You want the pain to stop. You feel like you no longer want to live.

After a week you too are also put on suspension. Now you are being investigated because you are his wife, and you are supposed to know him best. But you do not really know him at all. Now, not only is your marriage in jeopardy, but also your career. So, if you were this woman, tell me, how would you feel?

After confessing to my wife and finally managing to calm her I felt a weight being lifted from me. I was actually telling someone for the first time in two years that I was a drug addict. I also finally had the courage to tell her what I had been feeling for so long but could never bring myself to tell her. It was then that I realized I should have been truthful years ago, before my life became unmanageable and before I started hating myself for not letting others know how depressed I really was. I only needed to speak the truth. By not doing so, I was violating my self-integrity more with each day that passed, eventually leading to self-hatred and the eventual self-destruction of my life.

It became clear to me that I only had one choice as how to deal with this situation. I had to be completely truthful. No more lies, no more pretending, and no more trying and stay ahead of everyone. I did not want to think any more about what to say and I was tired of trying to lead two separate lives. I wanted to speak freely and be completely open and honest about what I had done. Quite simply, I needed to take full responsibility for my actions. I wanted to face my mistakes like a man, not a coward. The more I told myself this, the more I came to believe I was onto something. It felt right.

I told Lyndsay I would be back soon as there was something I had to do. I called Sue and fully confessed as to what I had been hiding from everyone for the past two years. I then called the Nursing Director and asked if it was ok to come in and speak to her face to face. I needed to be honest. I needed to talk. I needed help.

I cannot express enough the gratitude I have for Jane, Sue, Dr. B and Dr. D. I will be forever grateful for the understanding and support they gave me during one of the most difficult periods of my life. They all knowingly gave their time, support and compassion to a colleague that had been stealing and abusing drugs for years. I have the utmost respect and admiration for them all and will forever be in their debt.

After fully disclosing what I had been hiding I left the hospital knowing I had left it all on the table. I told them everything, including, how long I had been using, how I covered up the drug use, and how I had kept it hidden from everyone. I had nothing left to hide, and it felt liberating. People finally knew what I had been keeping a secret for over two years and a weight had been lifted from my shoulders.

I was informed that because of the extent of the stolen narcotics the police would be notified, therefore, charges would be laid against me. Only then did I realize just how serious this was. Not only had I lost my career, but I was also at risk of going to prison.

Over the course of the next two weeks I drank almost every day. I was in touch with all my family and friends and admitted to them fully what I had done. Then I simply drank vodka, smoked cigarettes, talked to a few counselors, and waited for the RCMP to come and arrest me.

The sound of a heavy truck pulling into the gravel driveway adjacent to the house and the slam of the doors caused me to rise out of the brief comfort of my patio sofa chair. The temperature was 24 degrees Celsius, which was unusually high for the month of July in Inuvik. I had just poured my third stiff drink of vodka, cranberry, with a splash of diet 7-up, and was about to indulge in a smoke to go with my drink, when I heard the footsteps of someone approaching from the side steps of the patio. The small dog we were sitting sprang into action, attempting to ward off the intruders with a series of snorts and grunts that resembled more of a sneezing fit than any actual attempts at barking.

This intrusion was expected, however, and my stomach began a series of flips, which turned almost instantly into a tight, nervous knot, and I knew they had finally come for me. I wanted to vomit. Instead, I took a final drink from my glass and I closed my eyes and pretended I was dreaming. I was not dreaming. This was happening. And I wanted another drink.

The two officers from the Inuvik police detachment barely acknowledged the little flat-faced furry creature, which, due to its failed attempts at intimidation had now become silent. Instead they focused on me, who was still holding a drink in one hand and a cigarette in the other.

"Hey Ben, you know why we're here right?" the shorter one asked. They did not need to introduce themselves, as we all knew each other; our professions deemed us to cross paths frequently. "Yeah, I do", I answered, and in fact I had been expecting them for several weeks now, ever since the letter was placed in my hands by the Director of Nursing a few weeks prior. "We need you to put your drink down and come with us," the taller officer said. I did not argue and yelled out to Lyndsay that I had to go down to the police station. They did not cuff me; which was nice, so I jumped in the back of the police truck. I was lead up the stairs of the detachment and placed in cells until the two officers were ready to question me. I did not realize it then, but while I was waiting they were in fact questioning Lyndsay in another room. I guess they had gone back for her and wanted to see if she had been involved in any way with what I had done. But she, like everyone else, had been completely fooled and knew nothing until I disclosed it to her myself.

Here I was again for the third time in my life, sitting in a prison cell facing serious charges. It was a lifetime ago when I was last arrested and I was only sixteen then and a different person than who I was now. I was a father, a husband, a university graduate, and an experienced ER nurse. I was also screwed!

I looked around at the names on the walls and realized I had taken care of most of these people as patients. It then occurred to me that this is where they went when I sent them to cells. For a second I thought about writing "Ben Cox RN was here" on the wall, but then quickly realized that was not at all funny.

They gave me the option to speak with an attorney beforehand, so I tried to call one but after waiting six hours and growing more and more impatient, I said to hell with it. I told the two officers I needed to make a statement and I did not need any lawyer there with me. I sat down and said, "I need to tell you both everything, and any question you have I can answer. I am the only one that can."

After several hours of pouring my heart out to these guys and laying it all out there, I was finally finished. I had taken full responsibility for my actions and was ready to face the consequences. They took my fingerprints, my mug shot, and gave me back my cigarettes and lighter. I left the detachment and returned to the house we were staying in. I felt free and I knew I was doing the right thing. It had to be right because it felt so good; I was proud of myself again.

After giving my statement I was officially charged with several offences and I was told I had to remain in the NWT unless given approval to leave. Lyndsay returned home to Halifax without me, her reputation still in question as the internal investigation continued with the hospital. She was put on suspension with pay until a decision was made as to her involvement in these crimes. But I was confident they would see the truth. I remained for another week and stayed with a friend of mine. I had managed to get permission from the court to attend a 30-day addiction program at the Northern Addiction Centre in Grande Prairie, Alberta. My start date would be August 5 and would have to include a week of detox prior to entering the program, which was mandatory. I had no offer from my employers to help with the cost, and I did not expect any. So with the help of my parents and the last of my money, I paid the six thousand dollar fee and booked my spot in the program.

On August 4 I boarded the plane that was heading to Edmonton, and after overnighting there, awoke early and boarded the flight to Grande Prairie. This would be the place I would live for the next 30 days, and though I did not realize it then, it would be the best decision I had ever made.

Detox? For how long?
Chapter 15

I arrived at the Northern Addiction Center in Grande Prairie on August 5, 2011, almost a month after being suspended from the hospital. It was during the weekend and the front doors were locked so I made my way around the back to the detox entrance. I buzzed the nurse's station and a voice directed me to wait until someone came to open the door. My only belongings were a knapsack with a few changes of clothes and my binder that contained my journal entries and the many phone numbers I had collected over the past month.

A friendly lady led me into a room and we began to fill out the necessary paperwork for my admission into the 30-day program. There was also a mandatory 5-day stay in detox for all new clients regardless of how long they had been clean. After searching my bag she led me to one of the rooms that had four hospital beds and gave me a locker to store my personal items. She then gave me a quick tour of the building pointing out the cafeteria, the workout area, the gymnasium, and where I would be staying after I was released from detox. For the next five days I was not permitted to be in any of the recreational areas and had to remain in detox at all times.

I asked her if there was anywhere to smoke and she pointed to one of the smoking corrals that was fenced in and monitored by video surveillance so I headed out and lit up a cigarette. The weather was beautiful and I could smell fresh cut grass that surrounded the building. I sat outside for some time just enjoying the summer air.

It was indeed a stark contrast to the early cold fall weather that I had left in Inuvik. A voice calling my name caused me to open my eyes and I saw one of the detox nurses standing by the door. She said it was time for my vitals, which were done frequently for the first several days until they could establish a consistent baseline for each individual.

I felt very strange being at the opposite end of a stethoscope as well as a little annoyed because the cuff was upside down and it was far too small but I said nothing. I decided then and there that I was no longer a nurse and no longer responsible for helping others. I needed to help myself, and I needed to let others help me.

Those first five days in detox were the worse days as we were pretty much confined to that wing of the building. Privileges such as the weight room and the gym were off limits and we were not allowed outside except in the smoking corrals. But that was the only fresh air I required.

I spent a lot of time reading and went through the three novels I bought at the airport within those five days. The staff kept us busy with lectures, videos, as well as mandatory Narcotic and Alcoholics Anonymous (NA/AA) meetings throughout the week. We were fed three square meals a day and I have no complaints about the food, as my appetite was better than ever. I guess it helped that I had been drug free almost a full month prior to coming since my only way to feed my addiction was from the supply at the hospital. Many of the other clients were not so well off and many were in full-blown DT's.

I could see the common symptom including the tremors, agitation, paranoia, diaphoresis, and restlessness. And that was just in the alcoholics. The hardcore drug addicts were often far worse, and depending on the drug and the degree of dependency, many clients spent several days in the ER prior to coming to detox.

But an addict is an addict, and all of us were here for the same reasons. One way or another we were all powerless over our addiction and our lives had become unmanageable. But first we needed to admit this to ourselves, which is in fact the first of the twelve steps to recovery.

As a smoker I am destined to become closer to other smokers than non-smokers. It is just natural as we have a general interest in the same activities. Most smokers tend to enjoy a cigarette in the morning with a coffee, after meals, when we are stressed, when we are bored, before bed, and if we want to get some fresh air. Basically we will smoke any time of the day.

I met a lot of interesting people in detox but there was one guy in particular who I really enjoyed chatting too. I had never laughed so hard in my life as I did when he told stories and I even asked him if I could use them in a book I was thinking about writing. Thankfully, he gave me his permission and I know I cannot tell them as well as he did, but here goes. I cannot use his real name as every client has the right to anonymity, so I will simply call him Andy.

These were a few stories told to me by my good friend and fellow addict, Andy, and if he ever reads this book I hope he will get in touch with me so we can talk. I tried to get his contact information from the addiction center but they would not give it to me due to some ridiculous "right to privacy" policy. Imagine the nerve of them trying to respect his privacy like that. In all seriousness though, I do need to thank him for cheering me up and taking my mind off my troubles during the first week of detox. I cannot remember the last time I laughed so hard and I hope he is doing okay. So, this is for my friend, Andy.

Andy Goes to Jail

This story takes place when Andy showed up at the Emergency Department and was in such a drunken rage that the nurses simply could not control him. The police were called in and they took Andy and tossed him in the drunk-tank with a bunch of Mexican workers who did not speak a word of English. He curled up in a ball on the dirty cement floor as all the bunks were full and then passed out.

While he was sleeping one of the Mexican guys decided it would be funny to clog the toilet with a roll of toilet paper and flood out the entire cell. Andy awoke completely surrounded by toilet water while the rest of the inmates were piled up on the bunks laughing hysterically at him.

One of the guards came around the corner and yelled, "What the hell is going on here? Who made this mess? The Mexicans seemed to know what the guard was asking them and they all simultaneously pointed at Andy who was still standing in the middle of the floor. The guard walked away mumbling something under his breath and returned with a second man carrying a fire hose, which they used to clean the cement floors when the cells were empty. One of the guards then said "OK then, if you want to act like animals then we will treat you like animals."

They sprayed poor Andy square in the face and the pressure of the blast took the glasses clean off him and knocked him to the floor. They then proceeded to blast the rest of the group, stopping every now and then to spray the floor as well as Andy. The cell was built for this though and there was a drain at the far end, which kept the majority of the water from spreading into the corridor.

After about ten minutes of being blasted with a constant barrage of cold water, the guards finally turned off the valve. Andy and about ten Mexicans were left curled into balls, soaked, shivering, and far more sober than when they had arrived. They were so cold in fact that they had to remove their water logged garments and huddle together in order to create some body heat.

Andy spent the remainder of the night almost completely naked, shivering, and the only white guy in the middle of a group hug with ten Mexicans. He said it was by far the most uncomfortable night he has ever spent in a drunk-tank. He was, however, much more fluent in Spanish when he arrived at detox the following day.

Andy Goes to Jail #2

This story takes place on a different occasion when my friend was again brought to the drunk-tank, except this time he was the only person in the cell. Now, Andy is a big whiskey drinker and if anyone knows anything about drinking whiskey you should know what it is to experience the "whiskey shits."

It is basically an uncontrollable urge to defecate and is usually manifested with tremendous abdominal cramps and explosive diarrhea. When it hits you it is unmistakable and you have to find a toilet immediately or else risk shitting your pants. When Andy felt it coming on he made a run for the toilet so he could release the immense pressure building in his colon.

However, when he finished and reached for the toilet paper he found there was none in sight. Andy began to yell out to the guards but after 20 minutes of unanswered screaming he gave up on trying to get their attention. He frantically looked around for something to wipe with but saw nothing. Then, a glance at his feet sparked an idea. He took off one of his socks and pulled it over his hand like a glove, then proceeded to wipe his ass until he was satisfied with the results. Desperate times call for desperate measures he thought to himself, then laughed a little and tossed his shitty sock in the garbage.

As time went on and hours passed his foot started to get really cold from the cement floor and he could not get comfortable at all. He needed something to cover his foot; he needed another sock to wear. He thought about the perfectly good sock that he tossed away which was fine except for being covered in shit.

Finally, he said, "Frig it" and pulled his sock out of the garbage can. He rinsed off as much of his own shit as he could and pulled the sock back over his foot. At least it was better than going barefoot and he lay back down on the bunk and fell back to sleep.

Andy's Brother Goes to Jail

This is a story Andy told about his brother's visit to jail and I cannot use his real name so let me just call him, Sandy. This was Sandy's first real jail term in real prison where, when you first arrive, the guards strip search you and then take all your belongings away. They then make you wear a standard pair of coveralls so every prisoner is dressed the same.

To figure out what size coveralls you needed they base it on your height and get you to stand against a wall to be measured. Now, Sandy decided to skip this step and instead just asked for the small ones as he was a pretty average height guy and figured they would suffice. But he was not short by any means nor was he thin like his brother and had a fair sized beer belly from years of excessive drinking.

He was handed the coveralls he requested and when he finally managed to squeeze into them they were so short he could not even stand up straight without the straps cutting into his shoulders. Also, the pant legs were hiked well above his ankles and revealed the majority of his knee-high socks. If this was not bad enough, the most uncomfortable thing was the severe wedgie he had from the inseam being pulled deep into the crack of his ass. Also, one could see the outline of his testicles, which were pulled tight and squished together on the right side of his coveralls.

The sight of this pot-bellied man trying to pick his wedgie out and shift his testicles around at the same time was just too much. The guards erupted into a fit of laughter and even Sandy could not help but find the sight of his own reflection amusing. After the laughter started to die down, Sandy asked politely if he could have a larger pair of coveralls to wear.

The guards looked at him and matter-of-factly said, "Nope!" and then pushed Sandy out into the general population and slammed the steel door in his face. Dumbfounded, Sandy slowly started shuffling past the other inmates as the guards all continued watching him from behind the glass.

Sandy and his tiny coveralls made their way toward the television room, reaching back periodically to try and remove the wedgie that was riding up his ass. He tried to sit but only managed to flump and lie straight on the bench. As he looked back toward the window he saw the guards all grabbing their sides and roaring with laughter at him.

Sandy vowed that the next time he went to jail he would allow himself to be properly measured prior to picking out his coveralls.

These stories and many others told to me by Andy kept me laughing for days and for that I am very grateful.

When the five days of detox ended I said goodbye to my new friend and joined the rest of the Business and Industry group who would be spending the next thirty days in the treatment program with me. I was very excited to get out of detox and get settled into an actual room with a door instead of a curtain.

The group including myself was very eager to have privileges such as restaurant and movie passes, using the weight room, running on the outside track, leisure activities, and access to the volleyball/basketball court. These were things that I had never really appreciated before but they certainly were a welcomed change after spending nearly a week in detox.

"What we do not resolve we repeat."

—*Sigmund Freud*

Thirty Days to Find Myself Again
Chapter 16

There were six of us in the new 30-day Business and Industry group and we were all working professionals whose addictions had caused our lives and relationships to suffer. It was a good mix of people, five guys and one girl, and she did not seem bothered at all by being outnumbered five to one. She fit right in with us and we thought of her more as a sister as the weeks went on.

I was in a room with three other guys and we got along great. They all had great qualities and I enjoyed each of them for different reasons. I cannot talk about their professions because it could easily identify them so I will just focus on who they are rather than what they do.

One of my roommates was big into running and he was never more excited than the day he was allowed to use the track. I joined him and another buddy as often as I could and discovered that I really enjoyed running with them. I could only do about eight or so laps, however, until I had to stop for a smoke break. They would both crack up at the sight of me sitting on the bleachers trying to catch my breath and smoke at the same time. They would usually continue until they reached their fifteenth lap and then join me on the stands. I was glad to have these two guys in my group because they motivated me to try and do at least some form of cardio exercise every day.

The weight room was always my preference though and I had made it my routine since Louis started taking me with him when I was up north. But the cardio was a nice change in routine. It helped me sleep better at night as well as gave me more energy throughout the day.

Those were my buddies with the healthy habits and then there were my other two friends. They were my smoking buddies, the guys I could just hang with and shoot the shit. They were both torments and kept me on my toes with their witty comments and constant goofing around.

One of them always looked angry and seemed as though he was always about to knock me out, but in fact he was one of the nicest guys I ever met. The other was a character for sure whose animated facial expressions could make you bust out laughing even when he was not trying to be funny. He would mess with me too and give me brutal riddles just before lights went out. I would spend hours lying there repeating the riddle over and over again while he would just smirk and then drift off to sleep.

One of his riddles was "The guy that made it does not need it; the guy who bought it does not want it; and the guy that has it does not know he has it. What is it?" After about four hours of thinking and staring at the ceiling, I finally yelled out, "I GOT IT!" I scared the crap out of everyone else that was fast asleep. When I told him the answer he was very impressed and told me that only about ten percent of people answer that riddle without some hint. Then he said, "Now shut-up and go to sleep you fool, we have an early lecture in the morning."

I laughed and replied "You're the one pretending to be the goddamn Riddler from Batman at twelve o'clock at night . . . riddle me this, riddle me that. I'll riddle you alright." We laughed for a bit and then I finally drifted off content with being one of the ten percent who solve it.

Our days were busy and the program required us to complete several larger projects as well as daily entries in our casework binder. The larger projects included a complete genogram and we had to describe the incidence of alcohol and drug abuse throughout our entire family tree. There were also several TTF letters or learning to "Trust Talking about your Feelings" letters, and they were very difficult to write. I wrote two letters; one to Mom and the other to Dad, each being about eight pages long.

I read the letter I wrote to Dad in front of my group and it was not an easy task. I was unable to hold back my tears while reading it as this letter described how much I missed him when he left and how hurt I was because of it. It felt good to get it out though and I even got to sit down and read it to him face to face when I returned home. It was very emotional and I am grateful that he listened to me; I know it was hard for him to hear. I read the second letter to Mom during family week and it was also a very emotional experience for both of us. A lot of the rage and anger I had held on to for so long came out as I continued to read the letter and again I felt a weight lifted as I read.

She flew all the way from NS to support me during family week as well as to try and learn more about what the program involved. It also gave her a glimpse into the lives and struggles of the other members of my group. She sat with me through several NA meetings and listened to me, as well as many others, speak openly about our addictions.

The only thing off limits to family was our group sessions where we met every morning with our group counselor. These sessions were much more personal and allowed us to get to know each other very well. We were pushed and challenged by our counselor and he never let any of us off the hook. He was indeed a master at looking through the bullshit. When he fixed his gaze on me and the corners of his mouth curled upwards I knew he was waiting for me to elaborate on something I said. I would feel him glaring at me in my peripheral vision and I knew he was not going to let me off easy.

He loved going after a few of the others as well, especially one of my buddies whose wits and sarcasm made him almost impenetrable to interrogation. He could burn you in an instant with the zingers that he let fly from his mouth like darts. Sometimes one would not even know they were being made fun of until hours later when it suddenly occurred to them and they felt crushed and inferior for not realizing it sooner. I think he was the only one who did not break down emotionally during the group sessions, meaning he was either highly intelligent or a complete sociopath. He was definitely one of the funniest, wittiest, and most genuine people I had ever met.

In addition to our group counsellor we also had to meet one-on-one with our case managers who helped us formulate a plan of aftercare for when we left the treatment center. She also happened to be very attractive and was a welcomed sight compared to the stocky, hairy, Stetson man that we met every morning in the group sessions. If I was a little less married, a little less of a drug addict, a little less unemployed, and a little less of a gentleman, I probably would have made a pass at her.

All jokes aside though, she was also attentive, supportive, empathetic, and genuinely cared for the well being of each of us. She worked really hard to help me prepare for court and hand-typed lengthy evaluations of my progress to provide to my lawyer. She allowed me to call the lawyer from her office and even took the time and effort to run down to our lecture room to tell me the lawyer was waiting on the phone. She really went out of her way for all of us and for that I will always be grateful.

There were also mandatory NA and AA meetings we had to attend which were open to the public as well as generic in-house meetings for clients staying in the center. Most meetings started the same with the serenity prayer and several readings from "The Big Book", which is sort of like a Bible for addicts. The floor would then be opened up for people to talk or someone would be picked at random to begin the session. If the person picked did not want to talk he or she could simply pass. For me, it was very hard to get used to talking in front of total strangers about the horrible mistakes I had made and how they had affected my life. But the more I listened to the stories of those around me the more I began to realize that maybe my problems were not as bad as they seemed. Many of the people who spoke had lost their homes, families, and health due to their addiction.

For many, these meetings were the only things they had to look forward to. It was often the only place that they felt like they belonged. In these meetings they could speak openly without being judged and without discrimination. It did not matter if they were a cop, doctor, stripper, gang-member, or homeless. It did not matter if they drank whiskey or beer or if they smoked crack or injected morphine because we all had one thing in common with each other; we were all addicts and we were are all powerless over our addictions.

I decided to force myself to speak at every meeting and to do it with complete honesty and fearlessness. I told those strangers about how I had a good upbringing and parents that never abused or neglected me. I told them how I was an excellent student and how my family and friends loved me. I told them that after my parents divorced I changed from a confident and outgoing boy into someone filled with anger and resentment. I told them about my drug use and past trouble with the law when I was young and how I got a second chance when my dad let me stay with him. I told them about how I went to university and became an excellent nurse like my parents both were. I told them about becoming a father and how unhappy I was in my marriage and my life. I told them that I was in fact worse than a street addict because I hid my addiction. I told them how less than a month ago I was in charge of the ER department in the isolated town of Inuvik and that I used my trust and the respect I had gained as a nurse to cover my drug use. I told them that besides losing my career and the respect of my colleagues

I also lost my sobriety and much of my self-worth. I told them I wanted to wake up from this nightmare and when I could not it made living with all the guilt and shame almost unbearable. I told them not to feel sorry for me because I did not deserve their pity. I told them how I felt like I did not deserve any help and that rehab was merely a break for me because the real struggle would start once I left. I told them about my fear of leaving and facing court and how I wished my stay there would never end.

I made it my goal, to speak in every meeting as a way of constantly reminding myself of what I had done and what I still had yet to face.

Apart from the difficult and emotional times there were also many good times during those thirty days especially when we were given group passes on the weekend. I know it must not seem like a big deal to most people, however, after spending two weeks inside the facility plus the first five days in detox, trust me, it was like winning the lottery when I got to go out. We went to the IMAX, ate at restaurants, hung out at the mall, went to the driving range, and visited Tim Horton's as often as we could. These simple things made us feel human again and confirmed that we were not just a bunch of addicts confined to a treatment center. It allowed us to feel normal.

We were also part of a fierce volleyball and dodge ball rivalry with the other group that was two weeks ahead of us in the program. They were a cool bunch of guys, mostly oil or mine workers from different camps in AB. They were like the cool kids in high school and we were envious of them because they always ordered out from the best restaurants. We also relied on them to show us the ropes and they mentored us on how to chair the in-house meetings once they left.

We all got along well but once we walked onto the volleyball court there was no love lost. They had a tough, young team as well as an ace power server who played in high school. When he served you only had a split second to react before the ball reached you. The less athletic players routinely suffered vicious blows to the face when they misread the trajectory of the ball. I have to admit that we usually got beaten but I also have to make known that the game was always close.

The last day before group graduation we planned a best three out of five-volleyball championship game. The winner would get bragging rights until the next time we all met in rehab, which was hopefully never.

While we were warming up and waiting for our rivals to show up we heard the sound of music coming from outside the gym. The other group entered carrying an old fashioned ghetto blaster from the 1980's and it was playing the theme song from Rocky called Eye of the Tiger. They had also found a toy WWE championship belt and their leader wore it around his waist as he strutted around the gym. They even stuck gold lettering stickers over it, which read "Volleyball Champions of the World" with a volleyball sticker above it.

It was one of the funniest things I had ever seen and we laughed and passed the belt around for at least a good hour. What impressed me most was the work and time these guys put into it and I think that besides being hilarious it was also their way of saying goodbye.

The game was really intense but in the end we could not dethrone the champs as they successfully defended their title. But we all had a good time and we did it without drugs or alcohol.

The next day they graduated and it was the largest attendance at any graduation in the history of the program. It was indeed a true tribute to how special this group of guys really was and I felt honoured to have known them.

One of the guys in the group had been challenged by another group member to stand in front of the entire audience and read the private letter he wrote to his family. This could not have been easy for anyone to do as I remember how I could barely speak when I read mine to Mom. I did not know what true courage was until I saw this tough, streetwise, oil worker muster the courage to stand and read to strangers his most personal thoughts. Everyone in the room, including me, was in tears as we watched this huge man, who was covered in tattoos, shake with raw emotion as he read his letter.

I knew that I wanted to be like him, I wanted that kind of inner strength; the kind that people cannot ignore. It truly defines what it is to be a man. Thanks "K" for your bravery. It was something I will never forget and I think it is safe to say the same for everyone else who was there that day.

I was very surprised at the graduation when they asked me to come forward and accept a cigar. It was a long-standing tradition to pass along a cigar to someone from another group when the most senior one graduated. The cigar is given to someone who they feel showed a willingness to work the program and recognized the importance that sharing with others had on their recovery.

I was honoured and thanked them very much and also informed them that I was out of cigarettes and probably not the best guy to give the cigar to considering it had to be presented to someone else at the next graduation.

At the very end we all lined up and took turns saying goodbye to each other. They ended up giving us the Volleyball Championship belt to keep in the building. They were a great bunch of guys and I hope they are all okay.

The meetings, the group sessions, and the volleyball games continued and pretty soon it was our turn to graduate. I had been drug free for close to two months now and alcohol free for over a month. I also felt and looked healthier largely in part to the three square meals a day plus the running and weightlifting.

Physically I felt really good. But mentally I was perhaps even worse than when I arrived. Do not get me wrong, I learned how to face my problems and acknowledge fully my shortcomings and admit that I was an addict. I was not afraid to speak in front of others anymore and I became used to telling people what I was feeling. However, while most of the clients who graduated were excited to return to their careers and marriage, I did not want to leave. I was the only one in my group who did not have a job waiting for me when leaving the treatment center.

Also, while everyone else's employers had sent them to treatment by with all fees paid, I was not. I was not offered any help by my employer and was left feeling betrayed by them. After all, that is what I was told when I got suspended. I was reassured that they would help me however they could. I did work for them for nearly four years. I was never in trouble before and prior to this incident my performance as an RN was immaculate. I was even told that I was considered by many to be one of the best ER nurses that the hospital had ever seen.

But if they did not offer me help, how could I ever ask them for it? The shame I felt for what I had done also left me incapable of asking them for help. So, here I was, on my own, cut loose by my manager and the majority of my colleagues.

It was also very hard to learn that a select few of my colleagues told the police they were certain I must have been trafficking the drugs as they would have known if I was using at work. Well, guess what? My own wife did not even know, the members of the RCMP I played cards with did not know, and my closest friends and family did not know. So it seemed to me that they must have formed these speculations to help themselves feel better for not noticing it sooner. It may have helped them sleep better at night if I had been selling the drugs rather than using it under their noses for over two years.

Anyway, I was on my own. I needed help. I needed to get better. And that is why I put myself in treatment. I had to help myself. I had nothing to lose, but everything to gain.

And there was still court to face and the possibility of a jail term was very likely. I was told by a member of the College of the Nurses of the NWT that because of my charges it was very likely a term in jail would have to be served. Thanks for the support pal; I really appreciated it. That definitely was not what I needed to hear right before I was to get on a plane to fly back to Inuvik on my own dime to face the community, the hospital, and the court. He probably should reconsider his line of work, because his empathy for people is seriously lacking.

Then the day arrived when it was our turn to pass along the cigar and the belt and say our goodbyes to the staff and clients at the treatment center. I had completed the program and was allowed to leave. My sister-in-law and her husband picked me up from the center and we all went out for dinner. I pretended to be better and kept up with the small talk but my mind was on other things that no one but me could relate to. I still had to face the real world and the consequences of my actions and I was no longer in the safe environment of the treatment center.

When it was time to leave, we said goodbye to each other at the airport and I boarded the flight that was heading north to Yellowknife, NWT. Here I met with a legal aid representative and entered a guilty plea to all charges. I did not know if I would be sentenced then and there or if I would be given permission to return home to see my family before sentencing. Nothing was certain with the exception of two things: First, I knew that the 30-day program gave me a new found strength and that I was never more prepared to face court. Secondly, I felt more alone than I had ever felt in my entire life and I knew that my sobriety could not last much longer. At least not until certain stressors in my life were finally laid to rest.

The judge in Yellowknife allowed me to return to NS until my sentencing date, which was scheduled to take place in Inuvik, NWT. While it seemed to me that the rest of my groups' recovery phase was well established when they left treatment, I felt like mine had only just begun. And for me, the treatment program was a mere vacation compared to what I had yet to face.

> *"You never know how strong you are, until*
> *being strong is the only choice you have."*
>
> —*Anonymous*

Please Someone; Help Me!
Chapter 17

Rather than talk about how I prepared for the days following rehab and what those three months entailed, I want to do something different. I want you to read the letter that, for me, was the hardest one I ever had to write. I wrote it one morning when I woke up and felt overwhelmed and alone with what I had to face. I was one week away from flying back to Inuvik to face sentencing in the Territorial Courthouse. Here is the letter, copied and pasted from my Hotmail account, which I wrote to my closest friends. It will explain everything that I was going through during this time.

January, 2012

One Week Prior to Sentencing
This letter is addressed to my closest friends and former colleagues; the people that I feel know me the best, have worked close with me, drank with

me, liked me and have been disappointed in me. I am writing to tell you all that I'm sorry for not being a better friend and for not keeping in touch more but if you know me at all you know I hate computers. Just know that everyone I'm sending this to is important to me and is someone I care about and feel comfortable being myself around.

I need to be honest with you guys about what I have been going through because these days I am learning that it feels good to tell people the truth. In the past months since I fucked up and threw away my career and admitted to my family and friends that I am an addict it has gotten easier to tell people what is going on with me.

I am not good at asking for help and most times would rather rely on myself to get through difficult times. Some of you can testify to this as many of you have witnessed me run around the ER like a madman rather than ask for your help. That is just who I am and I feel as though I am bothering people if I ask for help. But this is different. I am not well and these days I am feeling more and more overwhelmed by the reality of what I have done and have lost. I do not want to write this letter because the embarrassment I feel when I know I need to ask others for help is almost too much to bear but I know that sometimes the hardest things to say are the most important, so fuck it.

I have tried to do the right thing since leaving Inuvik. I completed the 30-day treatment program in Grande Prairie and did so out of my own pocket and with help from my parents. It was difficult going there from Inuvik as I just lost my job and wanted to be around family but it was worth it because I needed to help myself for a change.

Since returning to Halifax I attend NA meetings Tuesday nights and checks in with Pat, my follow up counselor from Grande Prairie, every Wednesday. I have also been meeting with Dr. Thompson who coordinates a support program for addicts in Halifax. I have been taking antidepressants for several months and feel better but life is still difficult and some days I have to force myself to get up in the morning.

I have been drug free since July 7th, the day my suspension letter was placed in my hands, the day when the secret I had spent two years covering up came out for all to see. I will not lie and pretend I am perfect as the stress and anxiety I feel about going back to Inuvik for sentencing often causes me to binge drink heavily, in an attempt to forget what I have to face.

The guilt and shame I feel when I think about what I have put my wife through also brings out an anger and self-destructive rage that I cannot describe and often am unable to control. What helps manage these feelings is to keep telling myself I am more than just an addict. I am a good father and have supported my daughter since she was born. I have never missed a child support payment and have never felt inadequate as a provider until recently as my EI payments only afford me to give my ex a fraction of what she was receiving when I worked.

I also believe I was good at being a nurse and worked very hard to help others. Dealing with traumas; saving people who were having heart attacks; treating and then sitting with patients that had attempted suicide; keeping homeless people overnight, feeding them in the morning and getting them out the door before shift change; putting a chart together and doing the admission assessment on a new admission that I felt bad about giving to the staff who were already busy on Acute Care but I was too scared of Nell coming on shift to keep them in the ER; going out for *smokes with Roger S. and Butch K. at night if they couldn't sleep due to withdrawals; blacking out at house parties and having to get IV boluses because I was slipping in and out of consciousness (thanks again for saving my life; you know who you are); walking through the screen door at the cottage the night after my wedding and getting videotaped doing karate in the living room (Jen Picek, my life goal remains to destroy that video); injecting myself with morphine one day because I was curious, unhappy, and when finding that it made me feel better deciding to do it everyday at work even on my days off but never telling anyone; constantly trying to cover my tracks, still perform my job, and continuing to steal drugs . . . .that is me and a few of the things I've done during the last few years of my career in Inuvik.*

I am not perfect. Who can say they are? Only people full of shit. I refuse to let this mistake define who I am and what I have done with my life. Rather, I want to be known for how I have taken responsibility for my mistakes and how I can handle what is by far the hardest thing I have ever been through. When I admitted to what I had been doing, Jane and Sue were a huge help and the support from Dr. "D" and Dr. "B" made me feel I wasn't alone anymore. It felt so good to be honest and not have that weight on my shoulders and I continued that path when the RCMP arrested me outside my nurse manager's house.

Against the advice of almost everyone, I gave the police the full story and did not wait for a lawyer. How could telling the truth be wrong or hurt me anymore than it had? This may have been the second stupidest mistake of my life but I would rather hold my head high than hide behind a lawyer or claim that I was depressed and suffered from a disease called depression.

Fuck that. I know I was not well but I was not brought up to make excuses about something that I knew was wrong. Yes, I couldn't stop using once I started and thought about it every day when I was at work, but I chose to take that first dose, and, depressed or not, that was wrong!

However, when my contract ended and my employers no longer had an invested interest in me to get better I had never once heard from them again. Everyone in the treatment program but me was there because their employers had felt they were worth the $6,000 fee in order to get them the help they needed. The clients here consisted of RCMP officers, drillers from Fort Mac, business and finance geniuses, teachers, and even other nurses. All were there for drug problems but none were charged with any crimes, not even the nurse who was caught taking drugs from work, and all were going back to a probationary work period once the program finished. The more I thought about it the more I felt that the only reason I wasn't getting help or have a job to return to, no second chance at all, was because I happened to be on a contract. Once the contract was over I no longer had union representation and my employers who I have been with for almost four years now needed to distance themselves from me as far as possible.

Four years in Inuvik is longer than most of the full timers had been there and these were not two-week contracts. We lived there and signed a contract for 1 year but ended up staying for fourteen months because they needed us longer. Then we continued signing contracts for no less than 2 months and most for 3-4 months over the next 4 years.

Inuvik to us was a second home; we were a part of the community and liked it there. We did not work anywhere else and made close friends with many who worked at the hospital, as well as with their partners (that's a shout out to Louis, Jordan, Jeremy, Mel, Eric, Jon-Paul . . . sorry for all the hospital talk). We were close, and even went to some of your weddings (Cubaaaaa . . . good time for sure . . . Jeremy's purple feet, the "just one more drink" fiasco in the pool and the third degree burn on Mel's uncle's bald head were classics).

Some weddings we didn't quite make it to (sorry Louis and Kat, Jeremy and Lisa, and Jordan and Melissa . . . this was not planned and I will always regret not being there for the most important day of your lives . . . I hope someday when this is over I can make it up to all of you.)

The point is that I felt I deserved better. Would the same treatment be given to a full time physician who had a problem? Have I been that horrible as an employee to not deserve help when I have never needed it more? I have even read a statement given to the police from Joanne stating there is no way that she wouldn't have noticed me if I was doing drugs at work and that no one could function while using the narcotics I was using. She told them I must have been selling them and that is how we paid for the many vacations down south.

Well guess what, Deputy Joanne? My wife didn't know and she lived with me! My friends didn't know and I was too embarrassed to admit to them what I was doing. The RCMP didn't know and I worked closely with them as we crossed paths frequently in ER and I was even using drugs when I played poker at their mess hall. I hid this from everyone because I didn't want to admit I had a problem and knew if it was discovered my career was over.

I was highly functioning and my tolerance increased but I tried to keep the doses constant to within a few hours apart. I also found that by only using it subcutaneously I was far less affected as it was slower absorbed into my system compared to intravenously. I used sterile 30-gauge needles to inject myself with because they didn't leave bruises or needle marks that my wife would have surely began to question.

As for the expensive vacations you accused me of taking, well which of the **TWO** might you be referring to? The one that we took to go to Wyman and Mel's wedding in Cuba, or the one to Mexico that my father-in-law paid for and brought us on for our wedding gift?

Only twice have I been out of Canada and when we went home between contracts we literally went home, to Halifax. Joanne has been to Disneyland or on a cruise just about every 4 months since she moved there.

We enjoyed time with my daughter and with family and then immediately came back to Inuvik to work. I don't blame Joanne for feeling angry toward me and realize it can be hard to hear the brutal honesty of what has been going on under her nose but It's not fair to accuse me of things that I didn't do and I will not let myself take blame and be crucified for things that are unfounded and untrue just so she can feel better.

I am not a dealer and if I was then someone would know it. I didn't hang out with crack addicts trying to sell them drugs at North Mart and the only friends I hung out with on my days off were the people I am sending this letter too. I did not want anyone knowing what I was doing and everything I was taking was only going into my body.

On Jan 31st, I am going to Inuvik to face my charges and the consequences of my actions. I will arrive on the 29th and my court is the morning of the 31st at 0930. This is not a trial and I am there to be sentenced for what I've admitted to doing since I was suspended. I am terrified that the judge will not see the good in me and only judge me based on what I have done. I don't know if my lawyer is able to show the judge that I deserve a second chance because he is only the duty counsellor on that day for legal aid and I have not even met him yet.

If I am to protect myself at all I have to rely on myself and that means doing the hardest thing I have had to do and that is to ask for help from anyone who knows me. I don't want pity from anyone and anyone who wants to stay as far from me as possible, I understand, believe me. But I have the bad feeling that I am walking into a massacre and the stress of knowing I could be sitting in a prison cell in Yellowknife is more than I can bear.

I don't need a reply from any of you nor do I need you to be present in court. What I do need is for anyone that has ever known me or thought I was somewhat of a good person or nurse to please send an Email to my lawyer about what you thought of me as a person and as a nurse.

There is no one else I can think of asking that knew me better than the people I worked with for almost four years and I know your disappointment in me and what I have put my wife through has changed some of your opinions of me and please feel free to write those as well, I can take it. But I can't just sit here and wait to be sentenced without trying to let people know who I am. I am not doing ok and sometimes the burden of what I have lost and what I still have to face is crippling. I know you are not used to me talking like this but I cannot afford to pretend that everything is ok anymore because that is part of the reason I am in this position. I feel like if I don't at least fight for something then what the fuck is the point to this life?

I have lost so much that the reality of it is

almost too much to bear. I need to have something positive happen and I need to know that I have something left to offer and that I am remembered for being more than just the nurse who stole drugs. There has to be more than that which defines who I am and how you remember me, right?

So I will ask it again, please help me feel as though I don't have to go through this alone. For those of you who wish to write something to the lawyer about how you know me, the address is tracy _ b***@gov.nt.ca and if you don't get a reply then the fax # is 1-867-920-6***.

He will be in his office this wed afternoon (NWT time) and needs them by then in order to prepare the other lawyer who is representing me on that day (this will be the third duty counsellor I have had since I left Inuvik).

I am sorry to leave this so late but I woke up this morning and felt that I should at least ask for help from those who know me best. If any of you want to meet just email or Facebook me because I'm not sure what hotel I'm staying at yet but when I know I'll get the room number to everyone.

I don't know if I'll be able to visit everyone until after court because I need to stay sober and clearheaded for this but I promise if I don't go to prison then you're all invited to my room Jan 31st to celebrate a new chapter in my life and it may be the last night I will get to spend in Inuvik.

Again, I'm sorry for fucking up so bad and whatever happens I am very thankful to know you all and be able to call you all friends.

P.S. This is not a suicide note so don't worry about me. I wouldn't put my daughter, my wife, my family or my friends through that. It's not in me. I promise.

I'll see some of you soon and will try and stay

in touch more. Maybe even break down and get on Facebook. Thanks for listening.

Ben

A week after writing this letter I flew with Mom back to Inuvik to face the court and the community. I wanted to drink the moment I arrived but no matter how much I begged Mom to let me she would not give me her approval. And without that I could not drink.

The sentencing went on for days as all the letters from my friends, rehab, follow-up counselors, and so on, were read in the open court.

The crown prosecutors were looking for a jail term of at least eight months in the Yellowknife Correctional Center due to the breach of trust and the extent of the stolen drugs. They were well prepared with several victim impact statements from my manager, the pharmacist, and a few others. After several days of hearing from both sides, the judge looked at me and asked if there was anything I would like to say? I stood and looked at my mom then faced the judge, the community, and the police officers I knew well, and then began to speak. I spoke as if I was standing in my meetings; I spoke without thinking, I spoke freely and truthfully. I yelled, cried, cursed, and laughed, and the judge did not interrupt me once. Basically everything I have written about in this book and talked about in rehab was what I told the judge. I wanted him to see me for more than an addict. If he was going to judge me then he needed to know me.

I think he saw me that day and I think he understood what I had already lost. I think he saw in me remorse, anger, imperfections, pride, shame, guilt, but above all, he saw honesty. He saw a man that flew to attend court on his own dime, paid for his own treatment, and was prepared to go to jail as punishment for his crimes. But after hearing this man speak, the judge just could not extend the prison sentence I had already served. On February 2, 2012, I was sentenced to twelve months of house arrest followed by twelve months of probation. Even without permission from the crown to leave NWT, which they refused to grant me, the judge overruled them and told me I was free to go.

After I hugged Mom who was crying tears of joy, I gathered my things, shook my lawyer's hand, and mouthed the words "Thank you!!" to the man who gave me a second chance. I was free to go home!

Welcome to Facebook!
Chapter 18

When I returned home from court a lot of changes occurred in my life. I went back to live with Lyndsay for a short period but I knew it would never work out between us, not after realizing I was unhappy with her. So, staying honest with myself, I left my house and all my belongings behind and lived mainly in various motels around the city of Halifax, NS. I withdrew my pension and applied for social assistance as I was now on my own and without a source of income. At this point I knew I was going to focus on the only thing that seemed to help me, writing!

I had been writing the entire time I was living in hotels and I had almost completed my manuscript when Dad and Kara offered me a place to stay in the basement apartment of their house. I think they were worried about me being alone in a motel and I was happy to let them help me. It was during this time at Dad's that my sisters helped me set up a Facebook account and an email address, which I had never had before.

I knew I needed Facebook to help me find the people mentioned in the book, otherwise, I could not use their names. It also seemed like a smart way to share the link people would need in order to purchase the book online.

I did not know what I was missing until I started finding the many friends who I had lost touch with over the years. The support and love I received from those people really got me through a lonely period in my life and it was their company that gave me the strength and confidence to finally put the finished manuscript to print. It was also through Facebook that I shared excerpts of the book to obtain feedback from others. I was also able to share the link to the CBC interview I had done in Yellowknife, NWT, just weeks after sentencing.

For this chapter I wanted to share one of the messages of the hundreds I had with my new found friends and I only wish I had the room to put them all in. But I was told to pick only one, preferably one without a lot of cursing (sorry Dwayne and Tanya), so I picked this one. I left it in the exact form it was written so please ignore the grammar and spelling errors as it was meant to give the reader the feel as if they were reading it from my computer.

Jennifer and I were classmates all through elementary school in St. Anthony and she was a very dear friend of mine that I had not been in touch with for over twelve years. It was great to reconnect with her again.

Jennifer

February 28

Ben Cox

hey stranger, just as i remember you. hope you are well you look very happy and the pictures are amazing, places you have been. good to see all the old gang again. been too long

Jennifer

Hey long lost buddy:)

Where have you been! Surprised indeed to hear from you today! Shocked actually. Thanks for the compliments Ben! I've been lucky and very fortunate to say the least. Your little one is quite the cutie and has her dad's blue eyes! Definitely been way to long. I think the last time we may have crossed paths was my grad or at Grenfell perhaps! I hope you're well and glad we've connected for sure. You also look great and very happy—you have a beautiful bride indeed. Way to go! Hope your folks are well and your brother jeff! Send my hello to the all and well wishes. Will you guys be making it home this summer for Come Home Year in St. Anthony?

Steve and I are planning on coming home—we are stoked!!!! Perhaps we'll see ya . . . . that'll be nice!

Be in touch for sure—sooooo nice to hear from you!

Ben Cox

i added you to a chat room. if you have time you should read my link. good to talk to you. i take full blame, I have never had facebook, email, or a cell phone and usually just lived for the moment. too many moves, too many new schools you know. anyway, see your still a Jordan fan. some things never change

Jennifer

OH MY GOSH!

*Seriously—you all right? Where are
you now? WHat are you doing? Is all
okay . . . How are you holding up?? How
is your family?? Seriously!! OMG!*

Hey man if you ever need ears or someone to
chat to you know you can reach out to us . . .

*I will definatly order a copy of the
book and spread the word if that is
what you are looking for . . .*

*I wish you and your family nothing but
the best and hope this is a thing of the
past and that only good things happen
from here on. I just shared your story
with STeve and we hope you are doing much
better and things are going well.*

*Keep us in the loop and be sure to stay
in touch . . . I hope that you know were
here and have family and friends that
have been through similar addictions and
some that are still suffering and we are
proud to hear your in a better place.*

*Take care—from the bottom of my heart!
J23 (yes 30 yrs old and still an MJ fan:)*

Ben Cox

*you are cute. I am never better. I have not
been happy for a while with my life. Everytime
i move, i would simlply not look back. and i
had several identities, but no real friends
that knew me, because i didnt keep in touch.
I cant stay with my wife, not happy, so i*

told her what i should have tolde her 8 years
ago. writing the book is kind of like therapy
was. and seeing people like dick, mark, luke,
dwayne, u, monica, etc for the first time in 15
years has been what i was missing. i forgot who
that kid was, so the book starts off with me
trying to remember him and his adventures. I am
safe and i dont want to be a nurse anymore. but
i need to get some of this shit out. But i will
be ok, i am stubborn and i have good support.
i am at dads no in halifax. you dont have to
buy a book, but there is several chapters about
st anthony in it. i think you will appreciate
the honesty of its content. thanks jen.

Jennifer

You've always been stubborn! And I glad you
have supports! We may be old friends but I hope
you know that if you ever need anything . . .
I am here:) For sure . . . I've looked for
you on here a few times as I am sure many of
the old gang have. We've spoke of you often
and hope nothing but the best for ya Ben!

Say hi to your Dad! How's Jeff and your ma?

So how long til this book is
published? Can we download it on to
our e-reader—I'd love a hard copy!

I am sorry you've been through this
Ben, but hope you know you always have
friends no matter how long it's been
or how far apart we've been . . .

Hearing your voice on the radio interview
was weird. But you've always been truthful
and real and tell it like it is. So I

am sure the book does the same and is
raw which will be intense I am sure.

Anyways—take it easy my friend
and be in touch:)

Cheers,

J23

March 13*th*

Jennifer

so when is this book going be ready for us?

Ben Cox

for sale?, ... a month at earliest . . . .
i have only two more chapters . . . . the
ending is done . . . . called "Welcome
to Facebook" . . . . includes actuall
conversations with those people i had to
call to get permission to use their names
in certain parts of book . . . . havent
talked to most in over 15 yrs . . . . its
realyy good . . . . do u want a taste?

Jennifer

absolutely—are you kiddin me??

Ben Cox

here are two . . . . and a bit about what
my wife at the time went through . . . .
enjoy . . . . let me know what u
think:) they are in your email . . . .
take your time i will be here

Jennifer

*HOLY SHIT . . . . THis brings me back . . .
OMG . . . this is freakin . . . this is
really freaking good Ben . . . WOW//Very well
written, easy, interesting and entertaining
read—delightful yet heartbreaking . . . . Your
emotions are raw and real and you put us in
that place with you at that moment, captures
the readers attention and is hilarious at
parts—I cracked up—OMG!!!!!!!!!!!!!!!!!*

Ben Cox

thank u jen

Jennifer

*And felt teary eyed at others because it
was sooooo realll . . . . Holy shit Cox:)
Well done . . . . Have you shared this with
others so far to critique . . . . ??*

Ben Cox

Yes . . . just a few

Jennifer

*Maybe I am biased . . . But this is
really good . . . . WOOOOOOOOOOOWWWW*

Ben Cox

i know . . . . i wrote it . . . . lol
Jennifer

*I can't wait to buy it an read it
all . . . I KNOW!!!! Well done . . . Pat
yourself on the friggin' back bud*

Ben Cox

i have!

Jennifer

Cause that's a job well done . . . .

Ben Cox

i appreciate it

Jennifer

and now i am clinging on the edge for more!
Lol . . . i was tellin nan and mom about you
the other day . . . omg—and the memories
that have you are hilarious:) Oh myyy

Ben Cox

thats what a lot of people
said . . . . they all want more

Jennifer

i know—I'll be patient . . . But seriously
holy shit—is it ever good, light and fun—
yet deep and raw:) Real! Love it . . .
Love it . . . . Love it . . .

Ben Cox

me too . . . its my life
Jennifer

seriously! you should considering writing . . .
I know you were doing this as therapy . . .
But hae you written anything else? have
you ever been interested in writing? or
just by chance got the natural nack?

Ben Cox

*it is what i always loved . . .
writing . . . . i was always really good
at it . . . . at description . . . at
putting people where i want them . . . and
making them feel what i need them to feel,
what i feel . . . . its easy for me*

Jennifer

well you done that and one that well

Ben Cox

*thanks . . . . i think this
will be a great book*

Jennifer

Indeed my friend . . .

Ben Cox

*but it gets very real . . . . very
emotional . . . its what i felt . . . .
and what i said,,,, what i did . . . .
and nothing held back . . . . the full
truth . . . . only way i know how to write*

Jennifer

*You definately capture the readers attention
and put them right in the book along side
of you . . . It actually felt like I was
there . . . . Wow—even more excited now . . .*

Ben Cox

its hard to read jen im not the nice noy u knew

Jennifer

*really hope your doing ok Ben. I hope
this has helped _ I worry about you*

Ben Cox

*im good, but awake . . . . and angry at
myself . . . . but im very strong . . . .
very independent . . . . i like myself
too much to ever hurt myself . . . . its
not in me . . . . please dont worry*

Jennifer

*No—I worry about how hard this has been and
what you've been through . . . obviously you
are an incredible strong man, you've had a
vulunerable time in your life and I worry
about your family and daugher and wife*

Ben Cox

*i can handle anything . . . . nothing was
harder than leaving st. anthony . . . .
not even juvenile . . . . not even facing
jail . . . . not even telling my wife i dont
love her . . . . i am very self aware . . . .
and strong . . . . its ok honey . . . . im ok*

Jennifer

*I always have been a worrier and you
guys have been through alot . . . .*

Ben Cox

yes but i handle things better than her

Jennifer

Just know that . . . We've talked about you and know how strong and courageous you are but still—you've been on our minds . . .

Ben Cox

and this book will be hard for her to read most

Jennifer

indeed—i can't imagine . . . jesus

Ben Cox

i know, ido, and im sorry for worrying you guys . . . . but i cant hide anymore . . . . i have to do this . . . head on . . . . and move past . . . . i need to find happiness . . . . and i have talking to you guys

Jennifer

that's it though . . . the past is the past . . . the future is what you will make of it . . . . and your journey is far from over and i anticipate lots of goodness for you my friend . . . . People will say fuck you—You fucked up! But you know what—you're strong . . . You have lots of things to look forward too . . . the book is just the start

Ben Cox

but i need the past . . . . i forgot about it . . . . buried it . . . . i want it in my life again . . . it makes me realize who i am . . . . where i come from . . . . it grounds me . . . . and i havent been on the ground in many years

Jennifer

Have you been in contact with a lot of old peeps? Facebook is crazy eh???

Ben Cox

everyone! from every different province I lived in!!!!

Jennifer

for sure . . . crazy the memories that surfaced when you speak to old contact and remember things from your past . . .

Ben Cox

and none have spoke to me in years . . . .

Jennifer

For sure! Awesome to have that contact now eh???

Ben Cox

this is the time to release a tell all book . . . . if there ever was a time . . . . its perfect . . . . it inspires me

Jennifer

for sure

Ben Cox

lol

Jennifer

it needs to be out before CHY_COme home year

Ben Cox

it will . . . . thats the goal

Jennifer

*you actually should see if it is at
all possible to have done before
then . . . You will doo very good*

Ben Cox

*and then i will through another come
year party for me after house arrest*

Jennifer

*smart—social media will play a huge
role, as will word of mouth*

Ben Cox

*face book is the key . . . . touch a
button and my link goes to hundreds*

Jennifer

Viral!!!!

Ben Cox

*I hit share and it goes to hundreds . . . .
they touch a share button . . . .
and it goes to thousands*

Jennifer

*Once someone shares it—it spreads to
hundreds, thousands of folks . . .
lol . . . . yes sir—same thoughts*

Ben Cox

*i will handle media . . . well
used to it . . . . no fear*

Jennifer

It will do well, You will do well . . .

Ben Cox

im ready for something good

Jennifer

Your interview was SSSSSIIICCKKK

Ben Cox

thanks jen . . . . u liked it?

Jennifer

*but it was insane, real, emotional, hearing
your voice was crazy, Steve and I sat here
listening to it and we were in awe . . . . with
the truth, the way your presented yourself*

Ben Cox

great thats a huge confidence builder thank you

Jennifer

*how calm you were, how real it was,
how you must have been feeling*

Ben Cox

*it was from rehab . . . . learning
to speak without thinking*

Jennifer

we hurt along with you—but were so proud of you

Ben Cox

only the truth

Jennifer

It was pretty impressive . . . and I passed it along to mom to listen to and was on the line while she listened

Ben Cox

i know jen . . . . im proud of myself . . . . really . . . . i need to do this . . . . i refuse to hide . . . . its never been me . . . . and there are more interviews coming

Jennifer

OMG-i think i searched you for days after that . . . . and after that i started reading the articles . . . . and felt for you . . . and your family

Ben Cox

my voice isnt in those articles though . . . . shed me in far worse light . . . . that's what made me wan to do the interview . . . . needed to give my side of things . . . . and show that im ready to face my mistakes . . . . i needed ot show my true character

Jennifer

wished there was something we could do or say and didn't know what too . . . .

*I know—hearing your voice was good.
I don't know when i saw you last*

Ben Cox

*just be there like u r now . . . . thats
it . . . . i cant accept help . . . .
but i will share my life with u and
anyone else who wants to know me*

Jennifer

*we'll i am always here, I may not ever
know what to say—but for god sakes know
if anyone is here i am Ben for real*

Ben Cox

i know . . . . i can tell

Jennifer

i think it's important to share

Ben Cox

me too

Jennifer

*your words are your way of
sharing . . . . you are great at it*

Ben Cox

*And its very liberating when
there are no more secrets*

Jennifer

*i share and am very open about
everything . . . . fun how facebook
allows that . . . . I love pictures, I*

love people, I love stories that people
shared . . . I always have . . .

Ben Cox

yeah . . . . way more confidence when u
r looking at a picture . . . . lol

Jennifer

I think that's why i am so intrigued by this

Ben Cox

well, i share just as well in public . . .
well used to it . . . . shit can i let u go
fer a sec jen, sorry can we talk later?

Jennifer

i am off to bed

Ben Cox

maybe give u one more bit to read tomorrow?

Jennifer

OMG_ for sure:) gimme a juicy
one!!!!! for sure . . .

Ben Cox

thank u, i really do appreciate it . . . .
your kindness . . . . i will, but you
will be shocked and cry . . . . sorry

Jennifer

Anytime ben, nice chatting!

We send our love:) Think of you often . . . . i am not ready to cry yet . . . lol . . . . see ya
Ben Cox

see ya, and u will cry . . . . because i did . . . and that doesnt happen much:)

"Sure as I'm breathing, sure as I'm sad, I'll keep this wisdom in my flesh; I leave here believing more than I had, and there's a reason I'll be . . . a reason I'll be back"

—Eddie Vedder

A New Chapter . . .
Chapter 19

The day I submitted my final manuscript for publishing a close friend of mine sent me my horoscope. I have never been a believer in this kind of thing and was about to delete it, when I started reading . . .

March 17ᵗʰ 2012

You are exactly where you are meant to be now, Capricorn, even if it doesn't seem that way to you. You may be feeling as though you made a lot of mistakes or missed out on certain opportunities, and that's what led you here. But whatever the reasons you are where you are now, there is an underlying destiny to it. Don't question how you got here, just rest assured that you are on the right path. You may feel that a change is imminent in your life, and it is. You are now in exactly the right spot to begin a transformation that will lead you to an important part of your wonderful destiny.

My books first arrived just weeks before the book tour was scheduled in NL. I had been staying in a dorm room at Mount Saint Vincent University since it was cheap and all the students were gone for summer. I was pretty happy when they arrived!

The marketing package came with posters, free E-reader cards, business cards, flyers, and postcards, not to mention 1,500 soft covers. Twenty-six boxes in total arrived at Dad's house and I only had a few days left before I had to cross on the ferry from NS to NL.

My first set up was in the library at Antigonish, NS. With
the help of some good friends from the nursing home
I worked at when I was in university, I sold almost fifty
books. By the time I finished signing them all it was only
hours before I had to leave to catch the ferry to NL.

A special thanks goes to the ladies from the RK
Macdonald Nursing home. I would not have had enough
gas money to get to the ferry without your support.

Matty P. and I with my rental car that was crammed with twenty-six boxes of books. Matt was heading back for Come Home Year in NL as well and he let me follow him on the trip just in case I got lost. I had not seen him since grade five. I said goodbye to Mom and we were off to catch the ferry.

We made it to the boat and after a night crossing we woke up in NL! I ended up selling over twenty books on the ferry and Matty and his friends thought that was pretty funny.

The ferry landed in NL at 7:00 AM and after driving eight hours we arrived in St. Anthony. I remember feeling very emotional as I saw this sign as a flood of memories started coming back to me. I pulled over and took a few deep breaths and tried to prepare myself for what I had yet to do.

After spending the night at my brother's house I got up the next morning and set up at the St. Anthony mall. I am so thankful for all the kindness and support I received on my first day. I met so many old faces and it felt so good to be home. I ended up selling ninety books my first day.

Seeing Dwayne, one of the best friends I had while growing up in St. Anthony, was by far one of the highlights of my trip. I visited his Dad and uncle too and seeing them again brought back many fond memories.

The breathtaking view from Fishing Point in St. Anthony. I spent a lot of time here with my friends exploring and climbing the rocks. This was the first time I saw it in over twelve years.

It was so nice here by the ocean that I decided to have a lunch break on the rocks. It was good to have some time to think and just relax before I had to go back to selling books again.

This was my set up outside one of the concerts during the St. Anthony Come Home Year. I did very well that night, selling over a box and a half. Eventually I got sick of sitting outside in the dark and brought my table inside so I could listen to the music while I sold books. There was a part of me that wished I could just have fun and forget the books but I knew I had to stay focused.

The next few weeks I spent travelling to every Come Home Year event around the Northern Peninsula. I lived in the car and not a day went by that I was not set up somewhere with my book. Here are some pictures of a few of the many places I landed . . .

Outside Western Petroleum gas station in Roddickton, NL, on a beautiful sunny day. I was not too picky where I set up, just happy to be in NL!

Outside Jim Randell's hardware store in in Bide Arm, NL.

Outside Michelle's Convenience in Englee, NL.

At the Come Home Year event in Griquet, NL.

At the mall in Corner Brook, NL. This is where I set up during the last few weeks of the tour and I ended up doing very well here. Makes sense considering it is the second biggest city in NL.

I met another local author while touring and he and I joined forces for a few events. Mr. Rex Saunders wrote about his near death experience while he was stranded for three days on an ice pan after his boat capsized. I really enjoyed his company and it was a pleasure to get to know him and his story.

Rex and I with a few lovely customers
at the mall in St. Anthony, NL.

A photo of me in The Northern Pen, the local newspaper
in St. Anthony. I sat down and did a full interview
with Luke Edwards. He was a great reporter and
did an amazing job on the story. Thanks Luke!

September 4, 2012, almost six weeks since I arrived in NL and I only had forty out of the 1500 books left. I was almost done!

And then there were none! After six weeks of travelling from place to place selling my book and talking to thousands of people, I sold out! With no books left and a rental car due back I booked the ferry to return to NS.

"What we remember from childhood we remember forever-permanent ghosts, stamped, inked, imprinted, eternally seen."-Cynthia Ozick

Thanks to everyone for your support throughout this journey and for making me feel at home again. I will miss you all very much . . . until next time!!

Acknowledgments

Thanks to you, Mom, for your never ending and unconditional love and support. If anyone has ever met you then they know that I am indeed one of the most blessed people in the world. Your ability to always see the good in me even when others do not has helped me through some dark times indeed. You are a strong, caring, and amazing woman, and I am so proud to call you my mom. "I will love you forever, I think of you always, as long as your living, my mother you'll be."—Robert Munch

Thanks to you, Dad, for being someone I can always count on even in the most hopeless of situations. I would never have made it through this and other trying times without your strength and support. Thanks for always letting me know you are proud of me and for never giving up on me. I love you Dad.

Thanks to my stepmom for always treating me like a son. You always believed in me and have always gone out of your way to do whatever was in your power to help both Jeff and I. Most of the good things I have accomplished in life would never have happened without you and for that I am grateful.

Thanks to my late grandmother, Mama, who kept me company for the last few weeks I was waiting for the books to arrive. We shared Dad's apartment downstairs and I could not have been happier to share that time with her and those moments I will forever cherish. I was hesitant to let her read the book as I thought she would be disappointed but she persisted so I gave her a copy. After she finished it she gave me a big hug and kiss and said, "My man, I am so proud of you." That was all I needed to hear from her. I love and miss you Mama.

Thanks to my follow up counsellor, Pat, who read the excerpts about rehab and encouraged me with her positive thoughts. Thanks for listening Pat; I appreciate it.

Thanks to everyone who chatted with me and kept me company through all the months I was on house arrest and sitting alone writing this book. You do not know how much I appreciated just chatting to you all after all these years and just sharing a laugh or two. I lost many good friends during my sentencing and the divorce so just having a chat every now and then meant the world to me. There were too many people who I found and spoke with so I will just say thanks to you all. There were a few, however, that really held me together through some rough times. A special thanks to Mike & Liz, Deanza, Joetta, Russell, Justin, Andy, Jennifer W., Jerome, Jennifer H., Monica, Pam, Janet, Dwayne, Andrea, Tanya, Matty P., Mark R., Renetta, Jessica, Sarah, Jill, Lou, and B.J. I know there are probably a few people I am forgetting so please forgive me if I have missed anyone.

Special thanks to my beautiful sisters who set me up with Facebook and Hotmail, and showed me how to use my first cell phone. I love you both.

Thanks to my brother, Jeff, for his advice on marketing and publishing. Thanks also to both him and his wife, Christina, for letting me crash at their house for a few days when I first arrived in St. Anthony. Also, big thanks to my nieces for all the kisses and hugs when I was there; I needed them!

Thanks to my rental car for never letting me down during the six-week book tour adventure. I will highly consider getting a Mazda the next time I purchase a car!

Thanks to everyone in St. Anthony, Roddickton, Englee, Main Brook, Corner Brook, St. John's, the rest of NL, and everywhere else in Canada and the world who bought a book either from me or online. Your support means the world to me.

Very special thanks to a very special woman, Angela. This new edition could not have been done without her help. Thanks for believing in me and standing by me through the times I had given up on myself. I am truly lucky to have you in my life.

I do want to thank another group of people who gave me the drive and determination to tell my story. I do not know them personally but they all commented on an online newspaper article about me. As I read the following comments I came to the realization that I had to write this book.

The following is the title of the online article and the comments that inspired me to keep writing.

'No jail time for nurse who stole drugs'

Read 5 comments

at 3:49 PM ET Just slap on the wrist!!! So much for our JUDICIAL SYSTEM!!! Agree with comment (3 people agree) Disagree with comment (2 people disagree)

at 7:49 PM ET Hopefully Mr. Cox will take advantage of this lenient sentence and turn his drug addiction around. People could have been seriously hurt, or even killed under his care. Does this mean he can still practice in Nova Scotia??? Agree with comment (3 people agree) Disagree with comment (2 people disagree)

at 5:34 PM ET Where is the picture of the person? What was the three year timeline? I think people in that area should know if they were treated by this person and when!!! Agree with comment (6 people agree) Disagree with comment (3 people disagree)

at 4:20 PM ET In Halifax doing WHAT? I hope not nursing!!! Agree with comment (10 people agree) Disagree with comment (3 people disagree)

at 11:25 AM ET And, I trust, he will not be allowed near any medical institution, or to practise as a nurse, ever again. I don't believe in stuffing people in jail unnecessarily, but some sort of very firm control needs to be put on this person if he is not to be confined . . . . Agree with comment (40 people agree)Disagree with comment (3 people disagree)

So, for those of you who are wondering what I have been up to since I was charged, well, I got honest. I put myself in rehab, faced sentencing, left my wife, lost my career and home, and wrote a book. And for those of you wanting to know what I look like there are many pictures of me in the book. I really appreciated seeing all your comments and I don't know if I could have finished this book without reading them…so thank you!